LORRIE ANDERSON

(Monchanki)

and

TARIRI

(Shapra Chief)

TRAILBAZERS FOR GOD

TRAILBLAZERS FOR GOD

This book may be ordered through your local bookseller, online, or writing to the following email address:

miguelvargascaba@hotmail.com

Dedicated to

all the young women and men

who desire to be

TRAILBLAZERS FOR GOD

For I delivered unto you first of all

that which I also received,

how that Christ died for our sins

according to the Scriptures

1 Corinthians 15:3

Foreword

Dear young women and men who desire to be Trailblazers for God,

The Lord is doing some wonderful things in this our 50th plus year of Wycliffe.

Wycliffe has now begun work with the Takashi and Michiko Matsumura, members from Japan, who recently made their first trip out to the 1000 Irarutu people of Irian Jaya, Indonesia.

There are an estimated 6000 Irarutu speakers living in the wide, flat jungle country west of Arguni Bay in the Bird's Neck region. There are two high schools, and the government is providing primary school education. All schooling is in Bahasa Indonesian, the national language of the country. While Indonesian is the language of education and trade, Irarutu is the language of the home and social interaction. We know the Scriptures will speak to them better in their mother tongue—the language of the heart—than in any other.

The Irarutu are quite different from the Indians among whom Doris Cox and I pioneered in 1950. The Candoshis were completely monolingual, understanding nothing of Spanish, the national language of Peru, not even knowing there was such a place as Peru. All they knew was "upriver" and "downriver." Some had been outside their area to trade and knew there was a city way downriver called Iquitos, where the "foreigners" lived. They didn't understand why we wanted to learn their language, but Chief Tariri decided we were harmless, and let us come and live with them—the first outsiders ever to do so.

The Candoshis were headhunters and constantly involved in intertribal warfare, so we expended a lot of energy the first few years just trying to keep peace. Since they were hundreds of miles from any medical facilities, we did a lot of medical work, and this opened the way into their hearts and lives. Learning their unwritten language monolingually and developing an alphabet for them was slow work, but eventually we did get all the preliminary grammar work done and translated the New Testament. In April of 1980 we had the joy of taking them printed copies of the Candoshi-Shapra New Testament. Besides

God's Word in their own language, they also have schoolbooks, bilingual schools and teachers, and there are probably 500 or more believers.

With the help of computers and other technical support, the Matsumura's task should be taking much less time. The rate at which New Testaments are being completed is accelerating. In the past 50 years, Wycliffe has finished 220 New Testaments in different languages, and our goal is to complete 500 more in this decade alone.

Wycliffe accepted 350 new career members this year, and we are encouraged to believe we may reach our goal of 3000 new members this decade.

I believe that you will be challenged to pray for the 300,000,000 people (the latest estimate based on new surveys) who still wait for God's Word in their language, many without any knowledge of Christ at all. I appreciate your concern for these "forgotten people" and your interest in Wycliffe's goal to get God's Word to every language group.

I would like to hear from you. The Lord's richest blessings upon you. Have a blessed Christmas season, and a year filled with God's goodness.

In His joy,

Lorrie Anderson

The Cost of a Translated Bible

How much does a Bible cost? I'm thinking about the REAL cost of a New Testament—one that the Summer Institute of Linguistics (S.I.L.) translates for a language group that has never had God's Word before.

The price tag on the Machiguenga New Testament was $23,455.00. There are even more financial costs, but I don't have the figures. It is the **TRUE** cost, however, that I'm thinking of—costs in terms of labor, emotional strain, health, even life. Only God knows the total investment, but here are some of the costs I'm aware of:

The Machiguenga book cost 25 years of work, and support, for Wayne and Betty Snell and their family. Then Harold and Pat Davis invested some years there, and later the Hamill family, all working with the Machiguengas in bilingual education and community development. It was team effort, and we must include the time and effort of typists, teachers, pilots, doctors, nurses, and other support people at the center. Add in two Helio Courier airplanes damaged beyond repair while servicing the Machiguengas. It begins to get almost astronomical (doesn't it?)

Then how do you add the emotional strain of separation from family and friends in the States, and from children they had to leave at the center for their schooling, or the physical output of hiking over dangerous trails for days? How about the lack of privacy? Or the exhaustion from nursing the sick people night and day when they come for medicine? Having to be available constantly (that costs too). And denying yourself any number of things to reach your goal....

Now let's run down the physical costs. Melody contracted polio out in the boonies—she's Wayne and Betty's daughter. Then the Snells had hepatitis, malaria, and amoebic dysentery, to name a few diseases. Some of the translation was done in bed—they were just too sick to sit up! And how about the commercial airline accident when Harold Davis lost his life on a return trip from Lima with a young Machiguenga man he'd taken there for medical treatment?

Now the sum of the spiritual *costs*—well, I guess God is the only one who can do that sum accurately. But living and working in Satan's domain brings incredible pressures and oppression.

Here are a few tag-ends that haven't fit in anywhere. Like the frustrating hours spent trying to crack the grammar. Or the hassles of bringing Machiguengas out of their villages, worrying that they are fed properly, feeling and sharing emotionally in *their* frustrations and discomforts, loving and hurting terribly when *they* hurt, or when they sin.

When you get all this down on paper, you wonder if anyone in the whole wide world is willing to pay the price! Or if that one who *tries*, has his head screwed on right! And you wonder at the audacity of a group like SIL (Summer Institute of Linguistics) who is out trying to recruit people to get this job done. "HELP WANTED" out in the most inaccessible, unhealthy places of the world. People needed who are willing to lay their reputations and lives on the line, people who are willing to work hard, who will part with their children for long periods of time, be available night and day for any emergency and be willing to count anything and everything total loss just so another group of people will have and be able to obey God's Word. But from long observation, I conclude these are the happiest people on earth.

Table of Contents

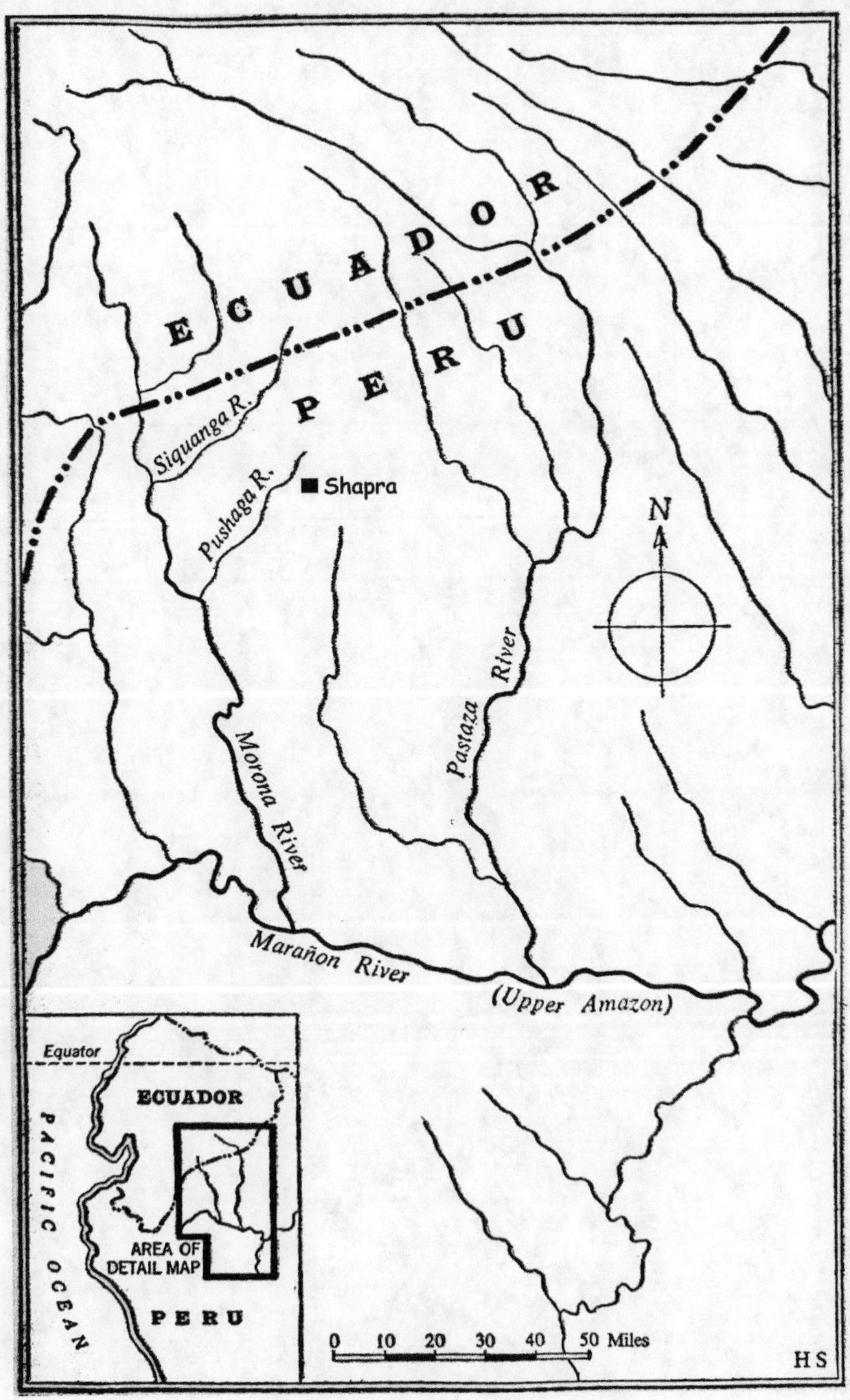

ECUADOR
PERU
Siquanga R.
Pushaga R.
Shapra
N
Morona River
Pastaza River
Marañon River
(Upper Amazon)
Equator
ECUADOR
PACIFIC OCEAN
AREA OF
DETAIL MAP
PERU
0 10 20 30 40 50 Miles
H S

Chapter 1 - Beginnings

This is a very good description of how the Jivaros and the Candoshi lived a century ago.

In the 1920s, an Anthropologist, Rafael Karsten, visited the Jivaroan tribal groups who live in Ecuador and in the Northwestern Amazon area of Peru. He wrote about them:

"The wars, the blood-feuds within the tribes, and the wars of extermination between the different tribes are continuous, being nourished by their superstitious belief in witchcraft. These wars are the greatest curse of the Jivaros, and are felt to be so even by themselves, at least so far as the feuds within the tribes are concerned. On the other hand, the wars are to such a degree one with their whole life and essence that only powerful pressure from outside or a radical change of their whole character and moral views could make them abstain from them." (Karsten 1923: 1-2).

The Candoshi and Shapra people live in that same area. Since their language was completely different from the Jivaroan languages, they very possibly migrated into the area between the Pastaza and Morona rivers centuries ago. They were also a warlike people but claimed that they learned the art of head shrinking from the Jivaro.

They believed in a Creator God who at one time visited their ancestors, but stopped visiting them when they did not obey him. At the time Lorrie and Doris first went to live among the Shapras, the people still believed that their God, Apanchi (our Father), still helped them and cared about them. They did not worship him they simply accepted him as an integral part of their lives.

Beginnings

I was 26 years old when I went to Peru as a missionary, and 28 years old when Uncle Cam (Cameron Townsend, founder of Wycliffe Bible Translators) sent me to bring the word of God to a tribe of headhunter Shapra Indians in northern Peru. My partner, Doris Cox, and I were the first team of women Uncle Cam sent into the deep

Peruvian jungle as missionaries. It was 1950. I would leave the jungle thirty years later.

Little did I know when I graduated from Ramsey High School in Ramsey, New Jersey, in 1940, that I would spend the better part of my adult life as a missionary. After high school, I worked for a parole officer, then took courses to learn bookkeeping, but I found I didn't like bookkeeping. My father wrote a column for the local paper, and I was interested in writing and wrote some poetry, but I could not earn a living writing poetry. I didn't know what I wanted to do.

I love nature and the outdoors, and my favorite childhood memories were visits to my grandfather's farm. I remember well the apple trees, the field and woods behind the house, the gray barn, the chickens, geese, dogs, and cats. God put a love of the outdoors in my life early, knowing His plan for me was to live the better part of my life in a very special outdoors place—the jungle.

Although my mother was raised in the Catholic church, our family did not belong to a church. I began attending a Presbyterian church with a friend, and I was introduced to missions through various mission conferences. I was enthralled by the missionary stories, and I began to know what I wanted to do.

The Lord led me to Providence Bible Institute, where I spent three years. I was accepted by Wycliffe as a missionary, and in the summer of 1947, I attended the Summer Institute of Linguistics (SIL) at the University of Oklahoma. I then attended jungle camp in southern Mexico, where I found my missionary partner, Doris Cox. My name is Loretta Doris Anderson. I was named Loretta after my mother, but I grew up as Doris. To avoid the confusion of two Doris's on a team, we decided on Lorrie for me and Dorrie for Doris. That worked well for us.

Cameron Townsend was expanding his translation work in Peru, and a base camp, Yarinacocha, was now the center of missionary operations there. Doris and I spent two years at the camp, helping where we could and waiting for our work as missionaries to begin in earnest.

From: Lorrie Anderson

Subject: Notes on initial contact with Candoshi-Shapra Indians (for the historical chronology of the Summer Institute of Linguistics, SIL, work in Peru.)

1. *Date of contact:* April 1950.

2. *Who was involved*: Victorino Gutiérrez, Harold Goodall, David Beasley.

3. *Mode of transportation*: Airplane. It would have to have been the Norseman, I think, to have carried three passengers, plus several weeks supply of food and such. (I guess the only other plane SIL had then would have been an Aeronca—the old Air Knocker, as Jim Price called it.) Pilot: Larry Montgomery. Who else? With only 2 planes and a couple of pilots, not hard to determine. However, at times my memory is sketchy. David Beasley can give you more accurate details on this, and other matters since he was there. He is the only living survivor of that survey team.

4. *Geographical location*: Survey was done on the Pushaga River, where the Shapras lived, I believe. Back then villages did not have names. And I'm not even sure it was in a village. There is a possibility that it was done down on the Morona. I have a vague recollection that Chief Tariri was not at his village and had to be called from/to somewhere else, after the survey team had talked to some of the other men first. (Good thing David is still alive, because I can only give you secondhand information, which after more than 50 years, is kind of fuzzy in my mind). I'm sure Doris Cox would remember some of the details, not only about this but, more importantly, about our initial meeting with Chief Tariri, and his people—no doubt some that I don't recall.

5. *Difficulties encountered:* Hostility from all but Chief Tariri himself. I don't know if the survey team were aware of it, but Chief Tariri told us about it. I won't go into those details now because it is, at least in part, hearsay. I'll write up an account of our first encounter as I recall it, and give you that, in case you want to include that also. I won't mind—well,

I will to a certain degree, but realizing that brevity is necessary—if you cut out a lot.

6. *Local language speakers involved?* Yes. Besides Cam Townsend, there were a number of other Shapra men there, as I understand it.

7. *Reception by the people*: Chief Tariri, friendly. The rest, lukewarm to hostile, probably.

8. *How long did the initial contact last?* Not sure how long they were there.

9. *Results of the contact:* Chief Tariri agreed to allow two white *señoritas* to come and live with them and learn their language. We were to go in July after they built us a house. Victorino stayed on to supervise the building of the house. When word came (I think possibly by radio through David Beasley, whose house was built first, several days away from the Shapra community) that our house was not finished, we said we'd go anyway. We could not wait. Doris Cox and I went to live in their community which consisted of 3 families. We went for 6 months, I believe.

Their reaction? All of the men except Chief Tariri were unhappy about our presence. They were curious, amused at our ineptness, but most of all distant and disapproving. The women were hostile, believing we were a threat to them—to their marriages. They thought we were fast women because we laughed, and smiled at the men, and talked freely to them, and looked them in the eye. And we were probably bringing all kinds of white man's diseases to their community. Only the children were open and friendly, especially the younger ones. (Some of the older children were sometimes disapproving of us, perhaps mirroring their parents' feelings.)

We felt that Chief Tariri's heart was prepared by God for our coming. He did not understand why we would want to come live with them, but he said, "I gave permission for you to come against the advice and objections of the rest of the men, because I felt you would bring us good." (There's lots more to this part of the story, but I'll leave it for a separate account of our part in the story, which I can't go into now.)

Chapter 2 - Romance

Yes, Lord

He was not the love of my life, but I thought he was at the time. In the mid-40's, while I was attending the Providence Bible Institute in Rhode Island, a friend and I were working a church social. We were sent out on the street to find members of the military to attend a church sponsored event for servicemen. Along came two men—one very tall and handsome—with blue eyes and a big friendly smile. His name was Glenn McKinney. I don't remember the other man at all. But we invited the two of them to the social, and they came with us and spent the evening. Later I invited Glenn to a dorm party at school, and he came. We had a nice time together, conversation flowing easily between us. I learned he was the nephew of B.B. McKinney, a hymn writer, whose name was in all the hymn books of the time. Glenn told me he was raised by his Aunt Bea on a small farm in Louisiana. And so, we had a short romantic friendship before he was shipped out.

I so looked forward to his letters, and we corresponded intensely. He gave his aunt's address to me, and I wrote to her. She invited me to come to Louisiana to stay with her for a few weeks. When I was coming back from a class at the University of Oklahoma, I stopped there. Aunt Bea, her husband T.J., and their daughter, Freda Katherine, gave me a warm welcome, and I had a wonderful time. Aunt Bea was a great southern cook, preparing delicious dishes from the fresh foods in her garden. I loved the farm. I could walk about and pick figs, berries, and other fruits that grew in abundance. Freda Katherine and I became great friends and are still friends to this day. She married and had five children, and we still sometimes catch up with a phone call.

Glenn must have gotten a kick out of letters from his home folks describing my relationship with his horse, Friday. I was not a confident rider, and Friday was not keen on me. When we took our first ride together, after a short while he realized it was his supper time. He took off for home at full gallop, paying no attention to my frantic efforts to control him. Somehow, I stayed on, but what a sight we must have been. Another time Friday and I went to round up the cows, about nineteen of them, I think. We got the cows back okay, but as we neared the house, a wind whipped up causing the clothes on the line to flap wildly. This startled Friday, and he veered away suddenly, and I went flying. The hospital said I was okay, but I might remember my fall for years on rainy days.

My long-distance romance with Glenn continued, letters flying back and forth between us. Once he sent me a dozen red roses, the only time in my life I ever received red roses from anyone. I was crazy about this tall, handsome, blue-eyed guy, and our relationship was serious.

One Sunday I attended a Salvation Army service. The following scripture was read:

Do not love the world or the things in the world. The love of the Father is not in those who love the world; for all that is in the world –the desire of the flesh, the desire of the eyes, the pride in riches—comes not from the Father but from the world. And the world and its desire are passing away, but those who do the will of God live forever.
I John 2:15-17

Then, very clearly, I received a word from the Lord: *Glenn McKinney is not for you.*

I was stunned, but to my astonishment, I was very calm. I didn't plead or beg the Lord to change his mind. I simply answered, **Yes, Lord.** It was a pivotal moment in my life.

Glenn and I continued our correspondence. I did not tell him of my word from the Lord, but over time our relationship became more of a friendship, than a romance. He must have wondered about the change in me, but he didn't ask about it. He came home, lived with his uncle, B.B. McKinney, and started college up north. I was accepted with Wycliffe and started my training at the University of Oklahoma. We kept in contact, but we knew we were headed in separate directions. When I reached Peru, I was so busy that I didn't even write very often.

In Peru, I lived in an apartment with girls who were with me in jungle camp. We were there to study Spanish. One evening we were sitting at dinner when I received a letter from Aunt Bea. She told me Glenn had married a girl named June. It hit me like a blow. I excused myself and, even though I hardly ever cried, I went into the bathroom and burst into tears. I had said Yes to the Lord. And now Glenn had said Yes to June. Glenn and Lorrie were over. I was surprised how much I felt the loss. *The Lord sometimes asks us to leave important things behind, say, Yes, Lord, and follow him.*

Chapter 3 - First Days

Missionary Recalls Year

February 3, 2016
Description of Shapra Indians

The Shapra Indians live North of the Marañón River.

The men wear home woven skirts and shirts. They like to wear feather headdresses. The women wear wrap-around skirts made of store-bought cloth and blouses like the Shipibos.

The men go hunting for food and cut down the trees and clear it for chacras. They make canoes, blow guns and darts. The men weave the baskets and go fishing and make the houses, too. The women clear the garden and pull out the weeds. They get some of their food from the garden. They spin wild cotton and weave skirts and belts for the men. The women fish and take care of the children while the men work. They make pots three feet tall for storing things. They make smaller drinking bowls that are made out of clay.

There are 60 – 70 people in each group. There is a head man in several groups. A chief leads the people when they go to war, and he listens to the people if they have any complaints against one another and acts as a judge. He is usually a witch doctor. To become the chief, he has to get the spirit of the jaguar, which is a big tiger. This makes him a good killer and not afraid when he goes to war.

When the Indian children are very little, they are taught to use machetes without cutting themselves and to cook in little pots on the fire without getting burned, and to sit alone in a canoe without falling out. Then when their front teeth come out, they have to start working. The boys go fishing with their fathers and help to cut down the chacras. They help to cook the food and sweep the house with a broom made of rushes. If they are lazy and do not want to work, they get spanked with stinging nettles.

Before the missionaries came, the people worshipped spirits. They were afraid of the spirit of the boa and the spirits of some big trees in the jungle. Now many of them are Christians. There are schools in three different groups.

The people keep parrots and other small birds and animals as pets. When the pets are very young the people chew up food and spit it right into the animals' mouths to feed them. They also have chickens, but they will not eat them as they are pets. They sell them to the traders. They always take good care of their pets. Some of the Indians keep cattle and are planting crops to sell. They also get money by selling animal skins.

The men beat drums and dance when they are drunk. The men have cow horns or large snail shells which they blow when they are quite far away from a village so that the people will know that they are not coming to kill.

Missionary Recalls Year
By Eppie Richbourg
Special Writer

Take one head.
Remove Skull.
Add herbs and bring to a boil over open fire.
Remove from heat.
Stuff with hot stones and sand
and set aside to cure.
Yield: One shrunken head.

Lorrie Anderson, missionary with Wycliffe Bible Translators, learned the above procedure when she became one of two women—the first Caucasians—to move in with a tribe of Peruvian headhunters more than 30 years ago.

It was a tough life, but Miss Anderson managed to keep her head and mercifully never was subjected to witnessing the shrinking procedure nor its results while spending the majority of her life with the Candoshi tribe deep in a Peruvian jungle.

Nevertheless, the first month with the Indians was no bed of roses, Miss Anderson remembers. First, the pilot who unloaded her belongings and set up the base radio neglected to install the transmitter, which left her and her partner cut off from civilization for a month.

"Somehow things got mixed up and the transmitter never got off the plane," she says, "so we couldn't contact our mission post. We could listen and knew they were trying to get us, but we couldn't answer."

"During the first day there, I was bitten by an insect and thought I was going to lose my leg from infection," she recalls. "But the Lord took care of me."

Why would a 25-year-old single American woman choose life among a tribe of headhunters? In today's world of female independence, the decision might not be mind boggling. But 30 years ago?

A talk with her reveals a type of bravery probably known to few women, But Miss Anderson admits her bravery was sort of thrust upon her.

"I didn't know the Candoshi were headhunters," she says with a shy smile. "A Spanish-speaking rubber trader named Victorino was the mission contact with the Candoshi. He had been a trader 20 years before and had never exploited the Indians as some white people had. He loved them and they trusted him."

Victorino left the rubber business and became a Christian, but never forgot his Indian friends, Miss Anderson adds. "He always wanted to go back and witness to them, but responsibilities of a family kept him from it. Later when he met Uncle Cam (a Wycliffe founder) he said, 'Would you send me some Bible translators up to the Shapras (a subgroup of the Candoshi)?' He said the people were very noble and hardworking, and he wanted them to learn about Jesus."

The missionary's recitation is interrupted as she becomes lost in memories of that world. Then she smiles, returning to the present. "Victorino omitted the part about their being headhunters and their drunken fiestas. I am glad he did, because I might have been reluctant to go."

Miss Anderson is a bit hazy as to how she discovered the Indians were headhunters. "It was more than 30 years ago and so much has happened since. I think we just got suspicious and asked. They said, 'Oh no, we don't, but the neighboring tribe does.' But then the other tribe told us, 'Oh no, we don't, but the Shapras do.' It turned out both of them did," she remembers.

"Later Chief Tariri told us he had a head there when we first arrived, but never let us see it because he was afraid we would be scared, which of course we would have been," she adds.

Why send women instead of men into such primitive territory? "Well, it just happened that way," she explains. "At first Uncle Cam got a lot of criticism from people who don't know the Lord." But he was vindicated, she adds. "Some years later, Chief Tariri told him that if two men had gone in, the Indians would have killed them. He said if a man and his wife had gone, the Indians would have let them stay a while, but sooner or later would have gotten into an argument with the man, killed him and taken his wife as one of theirs."

"But the chief said, 'Two women? What harm could they do? They're probably just looking for husbands.'"

"It was the Indian women who really resented us," Miss Anderson says. "They didn't want us there at all because they were sure we were after their men. They were the last ones to accept us. Once they did, they loved us, and the chief's wife became one of my dearest friends in the whole world—and still is."

Miss Anderson says some of the natives were puzzled for years as to why the two white women had come to live with them. "They couldn't understand the Gospel. The chief was the first who did. He seemed to understand when no others did. I think his heart was prepared for the Lord, because he said 'yes' so readily to our coming. I always felt he sensed we would bring progress to his tribe."

Chapter 4 – Lorrie's Life as a Missionary

SOUTHERN EVANGELICAL SEMINARY

LORRIE ANDERSON:
MISSIONARY TO THE SHAPRA INDIANS OF PERU

SUBMITTED TO
DR. WAYNE DETZLER
for
HISTORY OF MISSIONS
by
KATHRYN R. VOHS
NOVEMBER 19, 2004

LORRIE ANDERSON

Introduction

Ever since the first Christian set foot outside of the Greek-speaking world, translating scriptures into the mother tongue of the recipient has been the key to communicating Christ. Missionaries who have taken the great commission *"to the end of the earth"* (Acts 1:8) have sought to translate the Scriptures into Gothic (Ulfilas), Bengali (Carey), Burmese (Judson), Bechuana (Moffat), Chinese (Morrison), Algonquin (Eliot), Persian (Martyn), Korean (Ross), and many other languages, in an effort to reach people who have never heard of Christ. In this tradition, Lorrie Anderson sought to translate the Scriptures into the Candoshi language in an effort to reach each Shapra who has never heard of Christ.

Foundation
Growing Up

Loretta Doris Anderson was born on November 24, 1922, in Paterson, NJ. She was the eldest of three daughters and was called by her middle name, Doris. Doris was raised in a working-class home in Ramsey, NJ, and although her family did not attend church, she was sent by her mother to whatever church was nearby for Sunday school. At Sunday school, Doris never heard the Gospel except for in the hymns that were sung. One day, when Doris was 12, her regular Sunday school teacher was sick and Mr. Johnson, who was a born-again believer, taught the class. He gave a clear presentation of the Gospel. It offended Doris to hear that "all of her good works were only filthy rags," because she thought of herself as a "good girl." That summer, Doris went to a camp where they studied the Gospel of John for two weeks. On the last day, Christian cartoonist E. J. Pace spoke, and she decided to accept Jesus' offer of salvation and to dedicate herself to Him. She was given a booklet that had a prayer to pray and a place to fill in your name in place of "whosoever" in John 3:16. There was no follow up. Doris had no one to talk to about her faith and it did not grow.

In High School, Doris had a friend, Betty MacGill, who invited her to attend her church's youth group gatherings with her (several towns away in Hawthorne, NJ). Doris was usually busy with her friends, but one week, she decided to go. The youth group had a hundred members, and the church was full of born-again believers. It was what Doris had been looking for! A chance for fellowship and learning, growth, and affirmation (Lorrie always considered the Hawthorne Gospel church to be her home church). This church also had a substantial missions focus. They had sent out many missionaries and they often returned to speak to the congregation. At one such meeting, they gave an altar call for anyone who wanted to devote his or her life to missions. Doris went forward. At 17, she had set the direction for her life.

Bible School

Doris decided to attend Providence Bible Institute, in Providence, Rhode Island, in 1943, because she felt it would be good preparation for her life as a missionary. While at Bible School, she worked as a waitress. Many missionaries came to the school to talk about what they were doing. This is when Lorrie became aware of the tribes in South America which had never heard the Gospel, and she set her heart on serving them. Two of the missionaries that spoke at school were George Cowan and Marianna Slocum, of the Wycliffe Bible Translators (WBT). They spoke about the work they were doing with the various language groups in Mexico (the only country WBT was in at the time). Doris was very impressed with them and their accomplishments. In the fall of her third year, one of Doris' friends had returned from spending her summer at the Summer Institute of Linguistics (SIL) and she raved about how what she had learned would save her 2 years in learning a new language when she went to another country. Since Doris was planning to be a missionary, she should consider going to SIL first. Doris took her advice and applied to SIL for the summer following her graduation from Bible School.

Preparation

After God had laid the foundation in Doris' life—a love for Him, an understanding of His Word and a call to the unreached tribes—He began to prepare her to succeed. God had shown her that He could provide the support and direction she needed. Now He was going to show her that He could provide the skills she needed as well.

Summer Institute of Linguistics (SIL)

Doris attended the Summer Institute of Linguistics for the first time in the summer of 1947. She studied phonetics, phonemics (preparing a scientific alphabet) and morphemics (extended grammar). This built into her the skills of being able to hear a language, break it down into its component sounds, write a symbol, and ultimately an alphabet for it. Doris returned to SIL several times. In the summer of 1948, she studied advanced phonemics and morphemics and on her first furlough, she studied discourse analysis. This built into her the skills of being able to study a language and discern how it is put together. The Candoshi spoke a language unlike any other known language. The best way to learn it was by living with them and being immersed in it. Later, after analyzing the grammar further, Doris found the tools she learned in discourse analysis to be very handy for unlocking the mystery of the language. Doris returned seven more times to SIL (using these visits to bookend her furloughs) to consult with the experts and work on her Candoshi language understanding.

Jungle Camp

Jungle Camp was a 5-month experience that each Wycliffe candidate went through prior to going to the field. Its main goal was to build new skills, survival skills. In the winter of 1947, Doris, along with about 15 other candidates, learned how to build a shelter, cook over an open fire, and butcher a chicken. It was the most fun she had had up to that point in her life. Jungle Camp was strenuous enough that those people who lacked the temperament to make it in the field usually could not successfully complete it. It was at Jungle Camp that Doris got to know Doris Cox and the two of them decided to be partners. However, there was substantial confusion caused by them both being called Doris. Someone suggested that Doris Anderson go by some form of her first name. She was nicknamed "Lorrie," and has gone by that name for the sixty years since Jungle Camp.

After completing Jungle Camp, Lorrie returned for her second time to SIL. This time the work was even harder and, with her departure date looming closer, she knew that she not only needed to understand it, but she needed to master it.

Peru

Lorrie landed in Peru on October 6, 1948; Doris Cox had arrived about 6 months earlier. When she got settled, she spent some time in Lima, the capital. She started learning some survival Spanish by living with a Peruvian family for a month.

Opportunities came up for Lorrie and Doris to go to other tribes where work had already begun, but they had set their hearts on going to a tribe which had yet to hear the Gospel. They had also decided to go to a tribe whose language was not akin to any other language. So, while they waited, they served as temporary partners with other missionaries and became further acclimated to Peru. Lorrie and Doris joined Esther Matteson for 8 months among the Piros. Then Lorrie spent several months with Gloria Gray among the Cashibos. The time in these tribes was excellent preparation. They saw God working to bring these people to Himself and the memories of this kept them encouraged during the early months of struggle with the Shapra.

The Shapras

While in Yarinacocha, WBT founder and director in Peru William Cameron Townsend (Uncle Cam) happened to meet Victorino Gutiérrez. Uncle Cam told him about the work of Wycliffe Bible Translators in Peru and Victorino was very excited. "You must take the Word of God to the Shapras. They are a hardworking and noble people." Victorino had traded rubber with the Shapra Indians about 20 years earlier (when he was not yet a Christian). Ever since becoming a Christian, he had felt the desire to take them the Word of God, but he now had a thriving business and too many family obligations. Uncle Cam told Victorino that he would send translators to work with the Shapras, and asked him if he would go with the survey team. Victorino excitedly agreed.

When Victorino and the survey team reached the Shapra tribe and contacted Chief Tariri to ask permission for two young women to come live with them and learn their language, Tariri said yes. There was substantial disagreement in the Shapra tribe with Chief Tariri's decision to allow the women to come to the tribe. The men feared that the women were a precursor to the coming of soldiers and men who would take their land. Chief Tariri countered that they were only women, what harm could they do, they were probably only looking for husbands. Later he told Lorrie and Doris that if they had been two men, they would have been too threatening and the Shapra would have killed them (just like the Auca in Ecuador killed the missionary men). If they had been a man and a woman, the man would have been killed and the woman taken as a wife. However, two women were viewed as not dangerous.

The women flew to the Morona River in July of 1950, and they were met by Chief Tariri and some Shapra in canoes. The Shapra were shocked by the appearance of the women in their long flowing skirts and were frightened of them. They thought they were goddesses. As the pilot unloaded the radio and supplies, the Shapra had never before seen so much "stuff" that had to be paddled the 9 hours upriver to where the village was. Chief Tariri gave the women Shapra names after two of his sisters who had died. Lorrie was called "Monchanki" and Doris "Mpawachi".

Dr. Kenneth Pike, chief linguist with SIL, relates a story of the cultural implications of this first encounter. "When Lorrie and Doris were first introduced to him, Chief Tariri thought that they 'laughed in his face' and 'tried to throw him to the ground.' Why? The women had been taught that they should be friendly to people in Latin America, to smile and to shake hands. But this was a jungle Indian culture, not Latin. And in some Indian areas a greeting may include a bow plus the lightest of touching of the hands. A "warm handshake" involving unexpectedly heavy pumping could threaten to throw one off balance-- either physically or socially. Furthermore, the kind of smile which is appropriate may be culturally conditioned. When greeting someone, the lips often remain closed at the sides, and the cheeks crease close to the lips. Tariri, when meeting the two friendly, smiling North American girls for the first time, could have taken a 'friendly smile' for a guffaw at his expense. For messages to be quickly and easily effective, they must be culturally incarnate. Similarly, the universals of kindness and of courtesy also need translation-incarnation into emically-patterned cultural molds."

The Shapra were headhunters, carefully removing the flesh from the beheaded skulls of their enemies, filling them with hot stones, and boiling them to shrink them. It took 10 days to shrink a head correctly. These shrunken heads were trophies. They used them as decoration in their homes and wore them around their necks. The Shapra were feared by the other tribes for their fierceness. Victorino did not tell the women about this head hunting, and he told Chief Tariri not to mention it to them.

Language and Culture Acquisition

The first two years with the Candoshi were focused on language and cultural acquisition. Both Lorrie and Doris entered the tribe with no knowledge of the language. The few words Victorino thought he knew proved to be useless. Fortuitously, the Shapra were outgoing and loquacious, so it was not a struggle to hear words. The difficulty came from trying to connect the words with meanings. When Lorrie and Doris were first arriving in the canoes, they heard Chief Tariri call out: "*Nani, nani, nani,*" and a small boy appeared on the riverbank. Lorrie and Doris decided that "*nani*" meant "come." They tried it out on the children, and it worked.

During their first weeks in the tribe, Lorrie and Doris learned the language and the words primarily from the children. The men looked at them with suspicion, and the women looked at them with dislike. Only Chief Tariri spent time with them at the end of the day to teach them, as he had committed to do. One day an older woman came to them and suggested they call the men "*wawa*". They did, and suddenly everything changed. The men relaxed around them, and the women became friendly. What was this magic word? "*Wawa*" means brother. With one word the women showed themselves to be no threat and they became accepted by the tribe.

Every time Lorrie and Doris learned a word that could be used to describe God, they made the effort to communicate this truth. When they learned the word "father", they said, "there is a Father in the sky". When they learned the word "made", they combined it with all of the nouns they had learned to say, "the Father made the trees, the Father made the people, the Father made you." When they learned the word "son", they said "the Father in the sky has a Son". Then they learned that the Shapra have a name, "Apanchi," for a Father God who created the world, and then left it. They also had a legend that this Apanchi had a son who came to live on earth but left after an old woman hit Him with a canoe paddle.

After spending two years with the tribe, Lorrie and Doris had enough vocabulary and grammar understanding to begin to develop a written language for the Candoshi. Using this language, Doris focused on translating the book of Mark, while Lorrie focused on putting Jesus stories into the Candoshi language. Lorrie would work with Chief Tariri to develop the story translation and, in doing so, Chief Tariri developed a deep understanding of the Gospel story. After each story was translated, Chief Tariri would tell the story the next day to the other men while they worked. This added the benefit of real-time evangelism by the tribe's chief to the translation effort. As Chief Tariri grew in his understanding of Jesus, he began to ponder in his heart that age old question of Pontius Pilate: *What shall I do with Jesus who is called Christ?*" (Matt. 27:22 ESV [1]). In September of 1953, Lorrie had left for furlough and Doris had just returned. Doris Cox asked Chief Tariri when he was going to receive Jesus and become a child of God. He accepted Christ; his heart was ready. From this point on, Chief Tariri became an evangelist to his own tribe, to neighboring tribes, and beyond. He stopped killing because "when you know God, you love." Following his example, there are now about 2000 born again believers among the Candoshi.

Lorrie and Doris followed the tribal pattern of going to bed at dusk and rising at dawn. However, as time went on, members of the tribe would come to their "house" to talk over problems and seek counseling. This was one of the ways that Lorrie and Doris built deep relational ties to other members of the tribe. They also joined in tribal activities like fishing and planting. They gave up their western-designed clothes for Candoshi style skirts and blouses. The Shapra considered them to be one of them. Whereas other western women could exhibit "odd" behavior (such as wearing knee-length shorts), Lorrie's and Doris' actions reflected on the tribe, and they were expected to exhibit Shapra modesty, even when they were in Yarinacocha.

Spiritual Warfare Challenges
Sickness
The living conditions in the tribe were quite difficult. Disease and death were a part of everyday life. Concerned family members often brought sick children to the chief or to the witchdoctor to "chant the boa"—to go

into a trance to ask the spirit of the great snake to stop harming the child. They would not readily accept Lorrie and Doris' medicines. Lorrie was adamant about not letting people hedge their bets by taking medicine and visiting the witchdoctor. She did not want people to believe they needed to go to the spirits.

Rachel Saint (one of Lorrie's temporary partners in 1952) tells a story of a mother who had brought a baby dying of a high fever to them. Lorrie called the doctor on the radio, and he advised aspirin. The mother refused the aspirin and instead wanted Chief Tariri to chant the boa for the baby. The chief met her request and started to chant. Lorrie kept reminding him that when his wife Irina was sick, he had asked God for help, she took the medicine and got well. Chief Tariri stopped his chant and advised the mother to accept the medicine. Rachel and Lorrie gave the baby the aspirin in the name of God and within half an hour the baby was better. It was a sign to the people that God is greater than the boa.

Malaria was endemic to the part of Peru where the Candoshi lived. Lorrie fought a constant battle with it. She had an attack of malaria every other month for 18 years. These attacks continued, though with less frequency in the remaining 12 years she spent with the tribe.

Showdown

In March 1956, Lorrie was a participant in a showdown between the power of Jesus and the power of the spirit world. Due to a lot of noise and disruption in the camp, Lorrie had gone down to a canoe to have her quiet time to pray and study. Without warning, a large anaconda attacked her. It bit her many times in the upper body and finally clamped down on her left arm and used that as the anchor from which it would wrap its coils around her—to crush her and ultimately suffocate her before trying to eat her. Lorrie's screams went unanswered by anyone in the tribe and no help arrived. The snake had a good hold on her and arched its back over her head in order to wrap itself around her body. Then it let go of her and slid back into the water. God had said, "Enough." Lorrie's temporary partner, Lila Wistrand, washed the blood off of her and dressed her wounds. There was a substantial level of chaos in the tribe. Some were in a flurry caused by Lorrie's injuries and others were trying to deal with some visitors from the Quechua tribe who had walked several hours—an old witchdoctor and his daughter-in-law. These visitors demanded to see Lorrie and would not take "no" for an answer. The woman walked over to her house and saw her being bandaged and then turned and walked away. The witchdoctor later told

Chief Tariri that he had called upon the spirit of the anaconda—the strongest spirit in the spirit world—to kill Lorrie, and he was unhappily surprised to know that she was still living. Chief Tariri interpreted for him that Jesus was far stronger than any spirit in the spirit world. What was meant for evil, God worked for good because many saw Tariri's example, and pondered the power of Christ, and His love for and protection of His children. Not too many months later, that witchdoctor died when a fish got caught in his throat, suffocating him.

Spiritual Attack

Although Lorrie felt well-prepared by WBT for some things, spiritual warfare was not one of them. Attacks took several different forms—oppressive panic attacks, fear, and physical and mental assaults on them and those in the tribe. Lorrie felt a keen sense of responsibility to solve the problems she was presented with even though they were often medical in nature and beyond her expertise. She saw that Satan was using this situation and afflicting people in order to distract and discourage her. Members of the tribe would start ranting for no reason. Lorrie learned to say, "I reject you Satan; you and your works. And I place this person under the blood of Christ," and the ranting would cease.

Lorrie and Doris often found themselves in intimidating situations. Once, after they had just arrived, 8 to 10 whooping and hollering men in full war paint came to see them. There was no one from their tribe around and they had no idea what the visitors were saying. She and Doris contemplated running but they thought this would only result in their being chased. Eventually the men left. On another occasion, a happy party turned violent when they heard that Chief Tariri was going to ask for the beautiful young sister of one of the men there to be his wife. Doris misunderstood and thought they were fighting over them, so she and Lorrie ran off into the jungle in the dead of night (a definite no-no in Candoshi culture because it is deadly to be in the jungle at night). The next day the tribe was very angry with them because they had been afraid, and especially afraid of them. Lorrie and Doris thought they should leave and started to pack. Irina came over and Doris put her arm around her and said: "We love you." to which Irina replied: "Then you aren't leaving us?" Doris looked at her and said "No, we aren't leaving." and they started to unpack. Looking back, Lorrie feels that if they had let the fear win and had left the tribe, they would not have been allowed to return, and the door to the Candoshi would have been closed, maybe forever.

Translation

Although the translation effort began upon arrival, it really started to take off after Lorrie and Doris had been with the tribe for two years. They finally had enough understanding of the Candoshi grammar and vocabulary to discuss the Word of God with the Shapras. Lorrie's focus on translating stories from the Bible resulted in stories that were given to the Shapras as each was finished, increasing their knowledge and understanding of God and Christ. Doris' focus on translating the entire Book of Mark paid off when it was completed in 1956. After this, Doris permanently returned to the US due to health reasons. Lorrie had a succession of temporary partners until Beth Hinson was assigned to the Shapra tribe in 1964. Beth was part of the team until the 1980s, focusing on medical and educational work.

One of the more difficult words to find was the word for "faith." The Candoshi have seven words to describe belief—such as "I believe what you say"—but none of them carry the meaning of wholehearted trust that is in the word "faith." Lorrie and Doris finally chose a word that was used to describe a cooking pot that is leaning its whole weight on the log of the fire. The phrase became *magu taatokina*, "I rest my whole heart in," and because this depth of trust is not common in the Shapra tribe, it is mainly used only for Jesus.

John and Sheila Tuggy joined the Shapra tribe in 1959 with a specific focus on translation and literacy. Chief Tariri's half-brother, Shiniki, was the first Shapra to learn to read and he became the first teacher of the tribe. All of the children and many of the adult men went to school to learn how to read.

Lorrie was actively involved with the translation effort throughout the 1960s. In 1965, she accompanied Chief Tariri on his visit to the US. In the 1970's, Lorrie's time was split between caring for various family members with health problems in the US and working on the translation in Peru. In 1978, Lorrie and the Tuggys worked on the final revision of the Candoshi New Testament. When that was done, the Tuggys prepared it for printing. In 1979, Lorrie's father and sister both died. In 1980, Lorrie returned to Peru as the first copies of the Candoshi New Testament were distributed. They finally had the Word of God in their own language.

The Shapra People

The Shapra people, as Lorrie and Doris first met them, were a highly emotional people who deeply love their families. When a death occurs in a Shapra family, the women keen—a howling chant that eerily echoes through the jungle at night. The Shapra people were hard working. They were always hunting, fishing, planting gardens, harvesting palm hearts (and palm heart worms), making canoes, or building structures. The Shapra people were also warriors. They saw killing as an indication of manhood. They took the heads of their enemies and they lived in constant fear of being killed themselves. Chief Tariri was a "warrior" chief, a chief who leads the killing and who kills the most people. When he accepted Christ, Tariri gave up killing, and to a certain extent, his identity to the tribe and their surrounding enemies. "It is because Tariri loves God that he does not come to kill us," they said. "It is as if there were no Tariri. Even though Tariri was a killer, God changed him."

The Shapra people became a second family to Lorrie. She developed a deep attachment to many of the people in the tribe. One of her best friends was Irina, Chief Tariri's wife. He married her when she was young as his second wife (not her ideal situation). His first wife died of tuberculosis prior to Lorrie and Doris' arrival. So, when Lorrie and Doris joined the tribe, Irina was Chief Tariri's only wife. Irina had ten children, eight of whom lived to adulthood. When she married Chief Tariri, she did not love him; but when he became a Christian, they fell in love for the first time and acted like teenagers. At first, Irina resisted the Gospel for herself, even though Tariri and his son Tsirimpo were very enthusiastic about witnessing for the Lord. So, after a few more months of consideration, she came to the Lord. Lorrie and Irina spent time together every day, sometimes talking for hours on end. They grew to be very close friends as they went through the tragedies—the deaths of family and children—of life in the tribe. Irina shared all of her fears, like the fear of the other tribes attacking—which they did, shooting her husband and killing her brother. As a woman, she felt helpless to stop the violence around her.

Another member of the tribe is Yámpisa. He was one of Lorrie's dearest "sons". He was about 7 or 8 when she first came to the tribe. He would wonder and look up at the sky and think about God. His father was killed by enemies, so his family moved from the upriver Shapra group to Chief Tariri's tribe. He started school in the new bilingual school taught by Shiniki. He was the star pupil and became a teacher and pastor of the upriver Siquanga. One day a huge argument happened and Yámpisa became shamed. He gave up teaching and pastoring. For Shapras, when they are shamed and suffer loss of face, they feel they have fallen to a place from which there is no forgiveness.

Old Chief Shutka was the leader of the upriver Shapras and a cousin of Chief Tariri's. He had two sons, Pirocha and Pincho. When the sons were teenagers, all three of them took part in an attack on Chief Tariri, in which Tariri was shot and his brother-in-law Chiriapa was killed. Pirocha and Pincho lived in fear that any moment they may be hunted down and killed. However, Chief Tariri forgave them for the attack. Instead of taking revenge, he sent Yámpisa to the tribe to be their teacher and Pirocha and Pincho learned to read.

International Exposure

Unlike other South American converts to Christianity, Chief Tariri's influence spread beyond his own tribe, beyond his own country. In June 1957, Lorrie Anderson, Chief Tariri, and his wife Irina, flew to Los Angeles, where Chief Tariri was a guest on "This is Your Life", honoring Rachel Saint. Americans were intrigued by the former headhunter who had given up killing in order to follow Jesus. He was interviewed multiple times by newspapers and magazines, each time interpreted by Lorrie or Doris. When he was asked what he thought was the most interesting thing he had seen in the US, Chief Tariri answered that watching the multitude going forward to accept Christ at a Billy Graham crusade was the most exciting thing he had ever seen. He and his tribe had been praying for Billy Graham and the crusade in New York.

Tariri: My Story

For the 1965 World's Fair in New York, Uncle Cam planned to have a booth displaying the work of WBT and SIL. One of the things he wanted for the booth was a book about Chief Tariri. In order to write the book, Ethel Wallace sent Chief Tariri a list of questions. John Tuggy spent hours working with Tariri on this. Tariri responded to the questions on a tape recorder. Lorrie then translated his responses into English and sent the transcript to Ethel, who did not change it in any substantial way. *Tariri: My Story* was sold at the World's fair and beyond. It has found a special home with other tribal leaders in diverse places around the world. The issues that Chief Tariri wrestled with and the path that he took as he chose to leave the old ways and embrace Jesus, touched the hearts of those who are in similar situations.

One of the most touching aspects of the book is when Chief Tariri is talking about learning to read:

"I still don't know how to look at paper very well. When I have learned, it will be easy to tell God's Word. I will be able to say: "This is what God's Word says.""

"I am very sad about those who live bad. A lot of people lied about me. They kept lying and lying about me. So, I kept praying and asking God to help me. Then people stopped believing the lie. I told them how God helped me, and I told them we cannot forget God's Word. I said we should love God very much. God helps me very much. He does not just look on."

"As I heard God's Word, I thought: Why did they not come long ago? Why did they wait until now if they knew God's Word? There were many old ones, the ancestors, who wanted to hear.

I asked Mpawachi (Doris Cox), "Why did you people not come long ago? If you had told us long ago, the old ones would have known it, too. Why did God give His Book to you, and not to us?"

In 1965, when Chief Tariri visited the northeast for the World's Fair, in Flushing, NY, he was again greeted by a high level of interest. He was interviewed live by Barbara Walters on the Today Show. Chief Tariri answered her questions with his usual animation and made it a point to witness to the Today Show audience about how God had changed him.

The Work Continues…
The Luke Video
In 1994, Lorrie went to Peru to record a dramatic reading of much of the New Testament with four members of the Shapra tribe and John Tuggy. Later she was given permission to work on a video of the whole life of Christ from the Luke recording. Since preparing the Luke video in Candoshi was not a formal project, Lorrie did not receive technical assistance from JAARS at first. She worked for several years painstakingly trying to match the tape recording she had with the action on the screen. The project was finally finished at the end of 2003. In February 2004, Lorrie went to Moyobamba, Peru, where John Tuggy was working with three mother tongue translators. Each night a few of the 15 episodes were shown to the mother tongue translators and their families. They were very moved by the portrayal, especially of the Passion and Resurrection of Jesus. This was the first video they had

seen in their own language. Each of the translators got a copy of the video to take home and show to their own people.

The Old Testament

Several years ago, John and Sheila Tuggy began translating the Old Testament into Candoshi. By February 2004, the Book of Genesis was finished and in review. Lorrie hoped that Genesis can be recorded and used as a narration of a video of the key Genesis stories.

Summary

The story of Lorrie Anderson's work with the Shapra is the story of God's providence to bring a people to Himself. God found a young girl in New Jersey and brought across her path the people who would influence and inform her, teach and prepare her to go to a people who had not yet heard of God's grace and mercy toward them. At the same time, God raised up a chief in the Shapra tribe who was brave enough to allow strangers to live among them and who was interested in what they had to say about God. The more he heard, the more the words burned within him and the more his desire to know God—the God who was gently wooing him—grew. The result was a man completely sold out to his God, who evangelized the warrior tribes around him, and encouraged people around the world through his book.

Do you not say, 'There are yet four months, then comes the harvest'? Look, I tell you, lift up your eyes, and see that the fields are white for harvest. The harvest is plentiful, but the laborers are few; therefore, pray earnestly to the Lord of the harvest to send out laborers into his harvest. [6]

After Word

Meeting Lorrie Anderson has rekindled my hope that God has a future for me for which I am specifically suited. I had been held up as unacceptable for serving God, especially as a teacher, because of my gender. But here is Lorrie and all that she was able to do for the Candoshi was made possible because she *is* a woman. A man would not have been acceptable—he would have been killed before he ever could have begun. Only a woman could approach them in a non-threatening manner, learn their language, tell them about God and lead them to Christ. Without the women who gave up their lives in the US to have their lives among the Candoshi, all of the souls God saved in the Candoshi tribe never would have heard, and all of the people in the US and beyond that were changed by Chief Tariri's story would have been untouched.

Appendix I: Timeline

Foundation
Loretta Doris Anderson born in Paterson, NJ
1922
Lorrie accepts Christ
1934
Lorrie dedicates herself to Missions
1938
Lorrie goes to the Providence Bible Institute
1942

Preparation
Lorrie attends SIL I
1947
Lorrie goes to Jungle Camp
1947
Lorrie attends SIL II
1948
Lorrie arrives in Peru
1948
Lorrie and Doris go to the Shapra Tribe
1950

Language and Culture Acquisition
Lorrie attends SIL III
1953
Chief Tariri Accepts Christ
1953
Doris Cox completes translation of the Book of Mark
1955
Anaconda Attack
1956
Lorrie and Chief Tariri go to the US
1957

New Testament Translation
John and Sheila Tuggy join the Team
1959
Beth Hinson joins the Team
1964
Tariri: My Story is Written
1964
Lorrie and Chief Tariri go to the US
1965
Printed Candoshi New Testament is distributed
1980
Lorrie formally leaves Peru
1980

Recruiting and Preparing New Missionaries
1982 - 1992

Luke Video
Shapra record most of the New Testament
1994
Lorrie completes Luke Video in Candoshi
2002
Lorrie Visits Peru. Video is Shown
2004

BIBLIOGRAPHY

Anderson, Loretta Doris. Interview by author, 1 October 2004. Tape recording. JAARS, Waxhaw, NC.

Anderson, Loretta Doris. Interview by author, 8 October 2004. Tape recording. JAARS, Waxhaw, NC.

Anderson, Loretta Doris. Interview by author, 29 October 2004. Tape recording. JAARS, Waxhaw, NC.

Griffin, Robert. "Former Jungle Headhunter Chief Tariri Has Put Killing Behind Him" *JAARS Beyond* vol 17 no 2 (March/April 1989).

Pike, Kenneth L. "Christianity and Culture II. Incarnation in a Culture" *Journal of the American Scientific Affiliation* vol 31 (June 1979): 92-96.

Wallace, Ethel Emily. *Tariri: My Story from Jungle Killer to Christian Missionary*. New York: Harper and Row, 1965.

[1] All Biblical references are taken from *The Holy Bible: English Standard Version*, (Wheaton: Standard Bible Society, 2001).

[2] Kenneth L. Pike, "Christianity and Culture II. Incarnation in a Culture" - *Journal of the American Scientific Affiliation* 31 (June 1979): 92-96.

[3] Ethel Emily Wallis, *Tariri: My Story from Jungle Killer to Christian Missionary* (New York: Harper and Row, 1965), 83.

[4] Ibid., 79.

[5] Ibid., 94.

[6] John 4:35, Matthew 9:37-38 ESV.

Chapter 5 - *Nani, nani, nani*

I had been in Peru for about two years waiting for assignment when my partner, Doris Cox, and I were invited to tea by the wife of Cameron Townsend, the founder of Wycliffe Bible Translators. Doris (aka "Dorrie") and I wanted to work with a tribe without any written language, and there had been no openings as yet. So, we helped out where we could. I helped Esther Madison in the far eastern part of Peru, near Brazil, for about a year. There I learned to teach reading. It was when I had returned to Wycliffe base camp in Peru, that Dorrie and I were invited to tea. It seems Cameron Townsend had been sought out by Victorino, a rubber trader on the Amazon River in the Peruvian jungle, to see if there were missionaries who would be willing to go to the Candoshi-Shapra Indians in the northern part of Peru. It was a forbidding territory where no strangers were let in. The Candoshi people were notorious head-hunters known for their violence.

Soldiers, priests, and others seen as threats from the outside had been killed. But Victorino had found the Candoshi-Shapras to be a noble people and had grown fond of them. He had asked the Shapra chief, Tariri, if he would welcome missionaries who could teach his people about God and teach them to read and write. The two had a good relationship, and Chief Tariri had agreed, thinking this would be a good opportunity for his people. He said yes. The chief's word was law, so Victorino felt confident asking to send missionaries to the Shapras. So, over tea, Cameron Townsend asked my partner and me if we would be interested. We knew that we would be Wycliffe pioneers, as no other women had been sent into the deep jungle as missionaries. We responded that we would have to pray about it. When we had said our goodbyes and were safely out of earshot, we jumped up and down with joy. God had already given us an answer.

Our tea had been in April 1950. It was agreed that Victorino would go ahead to the tribe and build us a house. He would be finished with the house in July, and we would follow. A JAARS (Jungle Aviation And Radio Service) PBY Catalina amphibian hydroplane (a big 2-engined aircraft—originally donated by the Mexican government) flew out supplies, landed at the junction of the Morona and Amazon headwaters, where it was deep enough for the plane to land, and then everything was transferred to a canoe. This is the same path we would follow soon thereafter. It was a nine-hour trip, five hours by plane, four hours by canoe, and then considerable walking to the Shapra village. Dave Beazley went with the supply plane and took pictures to bring back to us. We thought the people beautiful and fell in love with their pictures.

Victorino built us a jungle-style house, a round structure on sturdy stilts with steps up to the floor. There was a thatched roof over rubberized sheeting, and we slept wrapped in mosquito netting in jungle hammocks. There was a private outhouse with a seat but nothing under the seat but a trench, and a private bathhouse on the river. These would be my jungle accommodations for the next thirty years.

We soon left base camp for the jungle, and during the canoe trip, Victorino tried to teach us some words of the Candoshi language. We finally landed on a beach where Tariri and some of his tribesmen were waiting. The people had heard the sound of the plane and knew that within so many hours the canoes would arrive. Chief Tariri would later say he thought we were goddesses. The natives were awed and scared, and some had their spears at the ready. In a show of friendliness, Dorrie extended her hand in welcome. The chief pulled his hand back quickly, for fear she was trying to lure him back to the plane. This gesture earned Dorrie an early reputation as a fast woman. Women did not reach out and touch men, nor did they laugh or giggle in public. These were all marks of a loose woman. We were beginning to learn the ways of the jungle before we even got off the beach.

Chief Tariri called out the first Candoshi words I heard spoken in the native tongue, words I will always hear in my memory: *"Nani, nani, nani!"* "Come, come, come," he called to his tribesmen, motioning his people to come help us carry our things to our house. Slowly, men appeared on the bank above to come carry our things. There were naked young boys, as boys do not wear clothing until they reach puberty. There were men wrapped in long skirts wearing seed necklaces with bamboo sticks through their ears.

They were a people as beautiful as we had seen in their pictures, with bronze skin and long dark hair. We followed them on a lengthy walk through the jungle to our half-finished house, set in a clearing. It was very private and quiet, and we had nothing ready to eat. It had been a long trip and we were tired. So, we put our things in some order, prayed with thanksgiving for our safe arrival, and crawled into our mosquito netting and slept in our jungle hammocks. We had a language to learn in the morning.

Chapter 6 - First Nights in the Jungle

Lake Capirona, Peru
September 7, 1957, Saturday
Dearest Family,

Lorrie and I are settled under our mosquito nets for our first night together out in Shapra-land! We left Base at about 8:30 a.m., after changing plans again not to try the Catalina. So, we took off in the Norseman (another amphibian aircraft, but smaller, with just one engine) and were able to take most of our original load, except another Shapra woman whose husband is a preschooler at the base, and her baby. Here is all who crowded into the cabin already filled with boxes, suitcases, duffle bags, spades, two metal folding chairs, and what have you. Irina (Tariri's wife) and six children, Lorrie and I, two white rabbits, two birds, two hens with setting eggs (one batch hatching out!)

We made two gas stops. All of the passengers except two became airsick. I shared my three Bonamine pills and couldn't understand why I hadn't brought more. At our last gas stop, all the Shapras stomachs had been quite well, emptied, and were getting hungry, so Lorrie gave them bread and hard-boiled eggs. She was so dizzy that she stretched out on the chigger-covered grass. I was hungry but couldn't trust myself to eat. Irina made *masato* for her family, mixing the prepared yucca (boiled and chewed) into a gourd (bowl) of water, and then everyone drank from it.

Our Norseman circled over Tariri's house on Lake Capirona to let him know we'd arrived so he could come down and meet us on the Morona River. The Norseman cannot land on small lakes. The pilots stopped by a muddy bank on the river where a small stream came rushing down. They unloaded all our gear in this God-forsaken green, steaming spot, and gave us a cheery goodbye!

When we started walking, we were immediately devoured by a swarm of tiny fleas. Horrors! My insect repellent was in the bottom of my duffle bag, but I got it! The children bathed, dressed, and then I gave them repellent too. Once our stomachs were more settled, we ate some of the wonderful lunch that Vera Borthwick and Jannie Townsend had made for us. About an hour later, probably around 3:30pm, Tariri and some other Shapra men arrived with four canoes to take our gear up the stream. It was finally loaded, including Tariri's heavy out-board motor (which had been given to him by a man in Lima). The rest of us hiked along the wooded path, led by Marachi, Tariri's oldest daughter (about 12 years old at the time). Irina, his wife, and her older friend Ishtiko, (who also came to meet us), chatted all the way catching up on the latest gossip (as told by Lorrie).

At one rest stop, I passed around Lifesaver candies, but Irina refused. She was crunching on a big hard-shelled black beetle. She looked more relaxed, peaceful, and happy than I'd ever seen her. All along the way, she kept poking around logs, or finding berries, fruit, etc., to eat. Presently we arrived at a small Shapra village. They were happy to see us, it seemed, but there was no robust, "slap you on the back" greeting. There was a girl with a three-day old baby in a cloth hammock, a flock of yellow ducklings, many skinny dogs, and a young wild boar that was tied to a peg under their roofing. After we looked around a bit, we crawled into canoes and paddled across the lake to Tariri's and Lorrie's place of abode. The men in the canoes with our load were not too far behind us. One of them reminded me very much of a Lacandon Indian from our Jungle Camp days.

The women liked my pink plastic belt that Elaine Townsend had sent out from Lima, when Allene and I were "babysitting" for her. It comes apart in sections and fascinated them. They felt my arms and hands and smiled at me, but I couldn't communicate with them. I want to learn Shapra too! When Tariri and his family ate supper, we heard him praying. Lorrie said that he told God he was happy to have his children back and that the plane didn't have any accidents.

September 8, 1957, Sunday

What a full day! Lorrie tried the radio to answer tribal rollcall at the base at 6:30 am. The generator and radio set were set up by Ralph Borthwick (our pilot), who was up here with Tariri and the Peruvian lieutenant, getting the .... [A few days of this journal are missing].

September 27, 1957, Friday

Helped Tsowinki and Ishtiko make the *masato* today, because the wife is ill. Yesterday, the men gathered the yucca (which is a real condescension for them because this is a "woman's job"). Then they kidded with us about us making the *masato* because they didn't think we would be willing to help with it. All we did was help mix it with a paddle after it was cooked. There is quite a system to making *masato.*

It is made from the yucca root (tapioca plant). The yucca, when grown, resembles the tall sumac bush and is planted in their fields, chacras which have been cleared from the jungle (the old slash/burn method). The root is then pulled out or dug up, depending upon the hardness of the soil. Then the top of the plant is cut off and carried off with the rest of the weeds that grow around out so that the field is cleared. The root resembles a huge, long potato. The skin is then peeled off and comes off readily after a couple whacks with the machete, as it is a sort of shell type. This is taken to the lake and washed, then whacked up into smaller chunks. Then it's placed in a big clay pot over the fire to which a proper amount of water has been added.

When the yucca is cooked soft, the really important stage begins. This is the thorough chewing of the yucca and the spitting back into the pot, mixing it all the while with a paddle until it reaches the proper consistency. Then they set it aside to cool, and from this, they make their all-important drink and food, *masato. Masato* forms the basic food staple of the day, provides the "cup" of hospitality to all who come, comforts the sick, and encourages the strong. It is always offered in a half gourd shell (various sizes), and by a woman, to the man, wife to husband, wife to guest, daughter to father or brother (etc.). When a man comes home tired from a hunt and his wife is out working, he will call her to get him a drink. He would never help himself. So, the woman not only chews it up for him, but also takes the pulp in her fist, adds water to the gourd shell and mixes it with her hands. Then she throws away the coarse, string-like pieces of *masato* to the dogs. She then offers it with all the dignity of Shapra womanhood. The *masato* is best when it is a day or two old and soured. In the former days, they used to let it ferment to the point of intoxication upon consumption. After all this, we made popcorn for the children.

September 28, 1957, Saturday

Lorrie and three of the children took crystoids against worms today, so they are pretty well knocked out for the day. I did the washing. Lorrie has a machine with a turn-by-hand washer. We set it and two tubs under the eaves of the washhouse (thatch roof only) to catch rainwater. We also made popcorn for the folks across the lake that got left out last time. The Huambisa man arrived in the middle of this process, and he was utterly intrigued by the process and the taste. I gave him some un-popped corn when he asked for some (probably to plant).

September 29, 1957, Sunday

Another very full day! We went over to Ishtiko's before church this morning to give them medicine, and then twice later in the day. Everyone is getting malaria! Right after our morning worship, the women said they were going into the woods to gather fruit and that I could come along. Irina and three of the children and I started down the lake in the big canoe. Her sister, Matarina and her son followed later. We paddled up to the bank under the overhanging growth of trees and bushes and started on our trek through the woods. It was dark and moist under the dense foliage. Part of the way was spongy and wet. It went up to my knees in mud in some places. The sun would shine through in places where the trees were further apart. The forest is quite a bit like ours back home in the US, just a few more plants native to the tropics, I guess.

We hiked and Irina felled two huge trees, and then we filled the baskets we'd brought with the tree's fruits. I attempted to carry one Indian-style on my back with a strap across my forehead, but had to relinquish it to stronger backs when we got to the swampy place. They insisted on helping me, and Irina warned me when I was about to hang on to a small tree-trunk that was swarming with ants.

This fruit is delicious, though like most jungle fruit, very little edible parts are obtained for all our effort involved. It has a huge pit in the center with a delicious, soft, yellow, mealy pulp around it which is about 1/8 inch. This also loosens the outside shell, but the Indians often scrape the shell off in the woods with their teeth before getting back home to cook it. It sounds for the entire world like horses biting corn off the cob (I don't mean that detrimentally in the least).

On our way back home, we paddled along near the shore, and they sighted a *majas*, an animal of the rodent family, about two feet long. So, we hurried back to our place of entry to get a spear left there, then combed the thickly wooded shoreline for about half an hour, sighting the animal occasionally, only to lose it completely in the end.

Tonight, the children wanted to play and sing songs, which we did with them in the moonlight in the big, cleared area between our homes. It is the mark of a well-kept home here, to have the grass cleared away and only show the bare earth. This impedes any small animals and reptiles, etc. from coming near the house. They spend a lot of time clearing the fields with their machetes, swinging them along close to the ground, cutting down the tiniest weed.

Then we sang songs for the children (mine in English), and the one they liked best of all was, "Fiddle-dee-dee-dee, the fly has married the bumblebee", because of its sounding somewhat like a bee, I guess, and also their word for bee is *mbimbi* (*mbeembee*). Then we had prayer with them and went to bed.

September 30, 1957, Monday

It's been a busy day caring for the sick! Tsowinki is worse. Baby Arosa (who went with Tariri and Irina to the United States for the TV program "This is Your Life") is getting too cute for words. She is walking really good and learning to talk. Once in a while, we have extra food which we give the children, and they bring their plates over. I've given Arosa raisins, and she loves them. Today I called her to see the little white bunny that sleeps in our house (given to Tariri by Bob Schneider, Wycliffe worker in Lima), and just said "*nani*" (come here). So, she comes bringing her empty plate stretched out in front of her! Way too cute for words!

The excitement of the day: Makowichi, the Quicha witch doctor who lives in this area and trades on the river, came to ask Tanchima for his sister, Mama, to be the wife of the Huambisa man who comes to us for shots. The Huambisa man is a peon of the witch doctor's father-in-law (who lives far upriver). Mama is a gay-hearted young girl, but has a hunch back, which is probably Pott's disease (TB of the back), which she acquired in her childhood. Every girl here is under the authority of her father, who consents to give her in marriage (she has nothing to do with it) or if he is dead, then the next of kin would.

So, her brother, Tanchima, was consulted for this transaction, but said "No", because she is an invalid, he said, (but mostly because he didn't want her to marry a Huambisa Indian). It is the custom for the girl to run into the woods and get caught easily by her "would-be" suitor, if she wants to marry him. However, even if she doesn't want to marry the man, she has to give up, because she is not safe alone in the jungle. So today, Mama ran into the woods when the conference began, and the poor Huambisa must be very squelched. Lorrie said if a Shapra is refused a girl, he will get so embarrassed that he will not show his face, or he will resort to killing the one who refused. What a culture!

It is really hot today, and the bugs are bad! We have an iron oven which we set over our log fire for baking. Today I burned a nice batch of brownies. Chief Tariri went fishing for two hours. It is so wonderful to see him recuperating so well!

October 1, 1957, Tuesday

The Huambisa man came back this morning for his daily shot in spite of being refused a wife yesterday. The Shapras would have too much pride to show their face again, Lorrie said. There is one bilingual Shapra who does all the interpreting for the Huambisa. The men got together again at Tariri's. Many are feeling better, and this is the first time the men have been together for a long time. The Shapras apparently bawled the Huambisa out, but all seemed to part as friends.

I had a good radio chat with Doc today about several medical questions after an unsuccessful attempt yesterday.

Mama was over for a long time today and had a good talk with Lorrie. The folks across the lake where she lives laughed at her and teased her too much about the Huambisa man, so she fled over here. Tariri was insulted that they would think of marriage when he was ill. Makowichi had come to Tariri's previously, and asked for Mayanchi, his pretty 11-year-old daughter, to be a wife for his 14-year-old brother. Tariri had just answered *wapa, wapa!* ("that's enough of that!"). He didn't say no, but simply said to stop talking about such foolishness. Mayanchi had run into the woods with Shutka, her younger boy cousin, who lives with them.

October 2, 1957, Wednesday

I can't even remember what season it is down here unless I stop and think. It must be beautiful in the States now. This was the last day the Huambisa man got his Reprodal shot for leishmaniasis sickness. We told him that he can come back home in a month when the plane comes with his medicine, as his case is so far advanced, he needs two treatments. I hope he does. He is in such a poor environment.

I went into the woods with Irina and three of the children today to gather palm-heart grubs and *chonta*, the delicious tender inside white shoots of a certain palm. Irina felled at least three trees and Shutka chopped a hole in the root end of the trunk of a huge, felled palm. It is fibrous inside the tree, and this is where the grubs live. There were only about twenty-four big fat grubs in this tree. They ate about half of them raw with great relish, and brought the rest back wrapped up in a big green leaf. Lorrie and I got one each, and roasted them. This time I ate the head and enjoyed it lots more.

There were about four different kinds of wild fruit that we ate along the way. We saw no animals and only one bird. It's amazing how these folks don't get lost. Irina chopped down one tree which was near a black ant's nest, and they started swarming over her legs and up the axe handle. She would stop every now and then and fight them off. How she could continue chopping, I don't know. I could hardly bare to watch it. These people all work like Trojans. I could never call the Shapras "lazy". Maybe some Indians are, but not these! They work so hard to obtain so little.

October 3, 1957, Thursday

Beth Eichenberger sent a message via radio today that she'd gotten a message from home to pass on to me. She said that everyone was well, and they sent their love. It was so good to hear!

The Huambisa man came back today bringing a chicken to help pay for his medicines, and is to return on Sunday with Makowichi's wife to talk about a settlement. This morning I helped Mayanchi prepare yucca for *masato* for Ishtiko and Tsowinki, because she is still ill. We peeled them and cut them up, then carried spring water from the creek where we bathe and filled their water containers. We also made these folks some jello, yesterday, and then oatmeal muffins today! These are the last of the sick folk. Tsowinki is much better, but has a persistent cough with purulent discharge (mucus).

Tariri and family went fishing and caught a lovely mess of fish. They gave us two and roasted them over the coals for us. Delish! I did a wash in the lake today, sitting on a log, projecting into it because we had no rain to fill our tubs. I lost a pair of tennis shoes somewhere in the depths. A deep-water search by the boys with a spear proved fruitless. I didn't know it at the time, but Tariri wouldn't leave and go fishing until I had finished washing, for fear that a Boa constrictor might come along.

October 4, 1957, Friday

This evening we had three surprise guests: Marashu, her son, Shimpotka, who is 14, and her daughter who is 5. Marashu was fleeing from her Peruvian husband who had threatened to kill his other wife (Peruvian) for infidelity. In the Shapra culture, two or more wives are legal, so to Marashu, her living with the man was legitimate. His name is Tsoplean. Marashu's other husband had been killed by the Ashuwaies after he had killed some Shapras and was fleeing from them.

Revenge killing is very ingrained in the Shapra and other Indian tribes' cultures here. Perhaps the initial killer may be a witch doctor, for example, who has been blamed for the death of some loved one, as he is believed to have power to cast a spell even unto death. So, the nearest male of kin to the dead one is by all proper respects obliged to kill for revenge. So, the vicious cycle begins. Then the nearest male relative of the witch doctor has to kill his killer or some of his relatives, etc. These tribal chiefs function mainly as war-chiefs protecting those under them from being killed and leading in revenge killings for them. The more killings he does, and the more fearlessness he shows, the more power the chief has.

This is one reason why Tariri had so much power and was so feared before, even now, due to lies spread about him. If you read the letter which I'd copied and which he dictated for Lorrie to send to Ralph Edwards, you'll remember he mentioned going to the Agarunas, a distant tribe, but in this area, for head hunting. It doesn't seem possible that the man I'd given penicillin shots to, sat in prayer, singing and Bible study meeting with, taken gifts of fish, etc. from, is the same chief mentioned above. I believe this is only possible by the power of the Son of God who lives in him, and has given him a new life. Maybe I should mention that women and children are never used for revenge killings. They may be taken as captives though.

So Marashu had been badly mistreated by Tsoplean, and was not only afraid to stay, but also hated him. She is a few months pregnant, which complicates her future. They'd paddled upstream for two days and were very tired and hungry. Tariri and Irina fed them, and they slept under their nets in our *sala*. The chief and his children went fishing today and shared two nice fish with us. They roasted them over the coals, just taking the insides and scaling them.

Chapter 7 - Early Visitors

Early Visitors

Doris and I had been with the Shapra people only a few days. Our house was still under construction, with half of the thatched roof, floor, and palm-board walls yet to be completed. I was outside reading, and Doris was busy with tasks in our half-finished house. We began to realize that we were alone. No one ever left the village without informing others of their intended whereabouts. No one had said a word to us, and yet no one was around, not even Victorino. He had not yet left for home as he was still busy with construction tasks. Even the dogs that patrolled for strangers and wild animals were missing.

We were puzzled and a bit concerned, but I went on reading my Bible, and Doris continued with her work in the house. She was the first to notice the bizarre sight approaching us. "Lorrie!" she said with great alarm in her voice. Running and leaping over the logs and stumps of a recently cleared patch of jungle came about a dozen young men headed directly for us, letting out blood-curdling whoops as they came. Their long dark hair flew behind them as they ran. As they drew closer, we could see red paint on their faces and bare chests, and sticks piercing their ears. Their white and black striped mid-calf skirts were rolled and tucked tightly around their waists. It was clear they were adorned for an event. We were terrified, and our prayers were flying heavenward faster than these men were running. When they arrived in our clearing, the young men ceased whooping and formed a semi-circle around us. We did not try to run, which would have been futile, and it may have sparked unwelcome excitement on the part of our visitors. We were immobile, frozen in fear, and praying hard for God's protection.

After a long moment, Doris had an idea. She went to her pile of belongings and brought back a camera. Very gently, in a calming tone, she explained to them how the camera worked, using motions and simple Spanish. Maybe one of them understood a little and shared with the others because they were greatly interested, and they passed the camera among them.

Doris told them she wanted to take their picture, and she motioned for them to stand closer together. The men must have seen this as a friendly gesture because with an ear-splitting whoop, they all jumped up in the air and came down in a close group. It was quite comical, but at that moment our pounding hearts let us find no humor in it.

Doris snapped some pictures, and after a few minutes of silence, the men let out another whoop, and jumping and turning in the air, they went leaping and whooping back the way they had come. Doris and I went limp with gratitude and relief.

What had just happened? Were these up-river men just curious about the white women who had come to live in one of the secluded villages of the Candoshi people—people who never let outsiders in? Had the men meant to harm us, but changed their minds? Were they simply showing off? Was this event staged to test our courage and character?

Later, people drifted back to the village, and life went on as if nothing had happened. Even Victorino had his story. He had been down at the creek working on our bathing area. He thought news of the two strange white women had travelled up-river, and these young men were just curiosity seekers. But why was the village suddenly empty, not even a dog around to bark at the excitement? Why were these men dressed and painted like warriors? We didn't know the answer to any of these questions. If this had been some sort of test, we just praised God that we seemed to have passed it.

Over the years we would not have answers for many things. However, we accepted the way things were, trusted God, and let Him work through us. It was we, after all, who were the visitors—strange and different as those men leaping across the clearing were to us. But we came to love these wild head-hunters of the Peruvian jungle, and most of them learned to love us back.

Chapter 8 - A Way of Escape

A Way of Escape

We were scared most of the time we were in the jungle, as there was much to fear—jaguars, snakes, malaria-carrying mosquitoes, and enemy attack. But we were never more scared than one night when we had been in the jungle only about six weeks. We still knew little of the language, and were still strangers to many tribal customs. We were in our beds, under our mosquito nets, while Chief Tariri was entertaining at his house a short distance away. There was much drinking of *masato*, dancing, and loud talk. Shapras were a loud-talking people, but this talk was louder than ordinary. I was watching it all between the slats of the wall next to my bed. Dorrie was fast asleep.

Chief Tariri had all the attributes of a great chief. He was strong, smart, fearless, a great warrior, a great hunter, and a great speaker. You would think any woman would want to be married to him. But that was not the case. His first wife had died, and his second wife, Irina, had a very beautiful younger sister, Tstsimari. Chief Tariri wanted her as another wife. The Shapra were polygamous, and there was nothing untoward about this. But young Tstsimari did not want to marry this powerful and intimidating older man, already the husband of her beloved sister, Irina. Her brother, Chiripra, and Chief Tariri were in a loud discussion about this marriage. Frightened and wanting to escape marriage to Tariri, Tstsimari ran out into the jungle alone.

The confrontation escalated to the point where the women gathered their young children and disappeared into the shadows. Suddenly, Chiki, the wife of Chiripra, came over to our house and ran up our back stairs. She entered, and when she stepped on the springy palm board floor, the movement awakened Dorrie.

Chiki grabbed Dorrie's arm in a vise-like grip, and began to chatter hysterically. Dorrie understood little of what Chiki was saying, but she screamed at me, "Lorrie, we've got to get out of here. They are fighting over us!" She feared some of the men wanted to marry us. I feared we would be injured in the violence that had erupted and wanted to get out of range. So, we ran from the house, barefooted and in our nightgowns, down the hill to our outhouse. Chief Tariri's crippled young son, Tsirimto, followed not far behind. He wanted matches to light torches to go into the jungle to search for Tstsimari. I returned to our house and gave him matches, and grabbed some for myself. Then, heeding Dorrie's frantic calls, I ran into the jungle. We continued running until we arrived at a small stream some distance away where Vitorino had built a platform across the water. It was the place where we bathed. There we sat shaking through the night, barefooted, in our nightgowns, on a platform in the middle of a stream in the jungle.

Morning came. We started creeping back to our house, hiding behind the huge roots of a fallen tree to make sure the coast was clear. We heard Irina calling us. Finally, we stepped out from behind the roots and saw her. She was so relieved to see us. She had been calling for us all night. We returned to our house where we were met by some children including their ringleader, Chief Tariri's young daughter who said, *Yotarittischa! Yotatoikcischa!* (You are bad! You are afraid!) Still shaken, we called base camp, and they said they would send a plane for us immediately. We began to pack our things.

We noticed Irina standing in our doorway watching us. Soon she was followed by others. They looked at us with pure disdain. They picked up items from among our things, looked at them, and threw them down as if they were contaminated. It is against the moral code of the Shapra to show fear, and they were disgusted to think that we would run away in fear. It was a tense and emotionally charged moment. Suddenly Dorrie put her arm around Irina and said, "We love you." The Shapra are an emotional people, and Dorrie's expression of genuine warmth diffused the tension. Irina said, "So you will stay?" Dorrie and I looked at each other a moment, and then we began to unpack our things.

Later, I wondered if Dorrie hadn't been right in her fear. The Shapra have a custom that if a woman is given in marriage by her father or a male relative, he expects a woman in return, or other compensation—a bride price, so to speak. Chief Tariri had no sisters or daughters of marriage age, so he could not exchange a woman for Chiripra's young sister. After Tstsimari ran away, perhaps we were being considered as a bride price to avoid further tension between Tariri and Chiripra. At any rate, the next morning when the alcohol had worn off and thinking was clearer, there seemed to be calm. Tstsimari somehow returned, and she eventually married the upriver chief's son. That evening when Dorrie and I had our evening devotions, we thanked our Lord for a good outcome to a very frightening time. Years later, I read a devotion that reminded me of our situation that day.

The Lord hear thee in the day of trouble; the Name of the God of Jacob defend thee; send thee help from the sanctuary, and strengthen thee out of Zion. We will rejoice in thy salvation, and in the name of our God we will set up our banners. Some trust in chariots, and some in horses; but we will remember the name of the Lord our God. They are brought down and fallen; but we are risen, and stand upright.

When the enemy shall come in like a flood, the Spirit of the Lord shall lift up a standard against him. —There hath no temptation taken you, but such as is common to man; but God is faithful, who will not suffer you to be tempted above that ye are able; but will with the temptation also make a way to escape, that ye may be able to bear it.

If God be for us, who can be against us? —The Lord is on my side; I will not fear.

Our God whom we serve is able to deliver us, and he will deliver us.

Chapter 9 - Life in the First Community

We didn't need an alarm clock. The Indians woke before daylight. The men competed to see who could get up first and dive into the river for their morning bath. So, there was much shouting and splashing and laughing going on early. Then shortly the whole community set off to work—to hunt, fish, build, or work the big gardens—any one of the many tasks necessary to a self-sustaining group of people in the deep jungle. The women would carry their babies naked in a sling, and the children would go to work alongside their parents, even the very young. For a good part of the day, we were essentially alone, except for an old woman and a very few others who stayed behind for one reason or another.

In the morning we folded our mosquito nets, dressed, and fanned the coals of our fire and built it up so it would not go out. Every house had its own fire, and if there were more than one wife in a house, each had her own fire and her own bed. The men kept wood by our fire and brought us water from the river that had to be boiled before drinking. We put water in a huge pot and sat it on three big fire logs to heat for our water needs for the day. Then we announced to whomever was present that we were making the necessary trips down a private path to our "outhouse" with its wooden seat that opened to the ground below.

This was a luxury. In other places, we simply had to squat and go on the ground. The announcement was necessary because whenever someone left the clearing he or she had to tell where they were going and for what, in case of danger. During the times when I suffered from malaria, I had to make this trip down the path many times. I would be so ill and weak that I sometimes did not have the strength to walk back to the house. I would lie down on a log to gather my strength to get back up the hill. The malaria was recurring. It came every other month on every other day for many years. When it struck, I would be sick with fever, joint pains, and headache, and all I could do was rest and wait it out. The traditional malaria medicines, such as quinine, did not work for me. After eighteen years battling this disease, malaria must have figured it was not going to get me, and so it left me. There were four different strains of malaria in Peru, and I had the cerebral form, *falciparum*. Unfortunately, when an Indian contracted cerebral malaria, they often went out of their minds and usually died.

Breakfast was usually papaya or banana and oatmeal. In our first house, we had a little table and benches at which we ate. It was not typical for the Indians to eat at table. The men sat on short benches or stools, and the women and children ate sitting on banana leaves spread on the ground. Sometimes the food would be dumped directly onto clean banana leaves.

After breakfast we had our morning devotions. The Indians who observed our prayers thought it quite curious for us to close our eyes and talk. They asked us what we were doing. It was hard to explain to them, as it took us about two years to know enough of the language to tell them the Gospel clearly. However, as soon as we could, we began witnessing. Even before we knew their word for God, we told them of a Father in the Sky who made everything—the sun, the moon, the stars, the plants, the dogs, and so forth. And we would tell them, God also made you.

We spent the day doing domestic chores, reading, and studying. A Shapra girl did our laundry for us, but she refused to wash our panties. She saw them as offensive and wouldn't touch them. The Shapra were a modest people. It was even considered immodest for a woman to show her armpits in a sleeveless blouse. When we discovered this, we stopped wearing sleeveless blouses. We bought cloth for the Indians to make us blouses in the Shapra style, a loose-fitting pullover blouse with three-quarter sleeves and a little button at the neckline opening. The men would bring back thread, buttons, and such when they went down the big river to trade.

When the Indians returned home, around 4:00 p.m., preparations for dinner began. The meal was food from the garden and some sort of meat—birds, fish, or small, clean rodent-type animals (not rats). Deer and tapir were not killed for meat because the Indians believed certain prominent people—chiefs and witch doctors, for instance, might be reincarnated as these animals. After Chief Tariri became a Christian, he said to me: "Go on the radio and tell them I ate deer"—this by way of showing he no longer believed in his pagan superstitions.

The men would throw down the catch of the day in front of the house, and the women got busy with it as soon as they had brought the men their cup of *masato*, a fermented drink made from yucca. The women worked hard. They were always busy, and their work was never finished. Sometimes they shared food with us, but we usually fixed our own meals. On occasion we would go with the women to pick berries and other jungle edibles that grew along the paths. We also went to the stream to fish with them. The Indians would dam up the stream and put a native poison in the water. When the fish were dead, they were scooped up and carried home to eat. If there were too many to eat at one meal, the fish were smoked over the fire and stored hung in the house for another meal. The same smoking process was carried out with other meats.

Around each house there was a very large clearing, which was swept clean every day. Any snake, tarantula, panther, or another unwelcome jungle intruder had no place to hide as it approached the house. The dogs were ever vigilant. The clearing around the house was kept free of debris, especially any form of food scrap which would attract critters. Children were punished severely for dropping animal bones in the clearing. Girls were punished more harshly than boys. Boys were prized in this warrior culture and usually received a sharp reprimand rather than physical punishment. One end of our square house faced Chief Tariri's house, and the other faced the jungle and our private path to our outhouse. Each end had a door. The door on the end facing Chief Tariri's house led to a large deck-like porch. After dinner, Chief Tariri and others would walk over to our porch to visit. The gathering on our porch was the evening entertainment—a place where ideas and stories were exchanged. It was here that we listened to the words of the Indians and began our dictionary of Shapra words and their meanings. Chief Tariri would point to something and pronounce its name for us, and we would record it. We were being schooled in the language at these evening gatherings, and our mispronunciations and misunderstandings were a great source of mirth to the Indians.

We followed a rotating work schedule. For six months we would be in the field, that is, in the jungle with the Indians. Then for six months we would be at Yarinacocha, our base camp, studying and working with the information we had gathered. Every five years we would have a one-year furlough to go home and see family, keep doctor's appointments, or do whatever we chose or needed to do. I spent two sessions at SIL (Summer Institute of Linguistics) in Oklahoma during my several furloughs. And so, the years flew by. Chief Tariri's group moved from place to place in the jungle, partners came and went, schools were formed, Shapra teachers trained. After five years, Doris went home ill and did not return. She was largely responsible for translating the book of Mark. Others took her place. And finally, after thirty odd years, the Shapra were largely a literate people. The New Testament was translated into the Shapra language, and was dedicated in 1980.

Chapter 10 - From Savage to Responsible Citizen

CANDOSHI-SHAPRA (Peru)
From Savage to Responsible Citizen (or Saint)
By Grace Watkins

May 6, 2016
Tariri, chief of a fierce tribe of head shrinkers, was accustomed to killing strangers when they crossed his path. But when two women, Doris Cox and Lorrie Anderson, arrived in his village, he thought perhaps they were looking for husbands, and he let them live!

The girls did not find husbands, but they brought the Word of God to this fast-dying group of Indians in Peru. Tariri was transformed completely, from a savage who avenged every death by killing, to a man who refused even to defend himself.

"I don't want to fight anymore," Tariri declared, as he set about making plans for a model village of peace and progress.

But when he felt a merchant in Lima who had sent him a motor for his boat had cheated him, he was sorely tried.

"You sent me a bad motor," Tariri dictated in a letter.

"I used to take off heads. When people would send bad messages to us, we would say, 'Because they want to die, they do that!'"

"Then Jesus overcame me. Even though I used to take off heads, I have quit doing so. Even though you sent me a bad motor, I love you."

Replacement parts of the motor were promptly dispatched!

The Peruvian government has now established schools among the Candoshi-Shapra people. Tariri's brother became a teacher, and his son became a teacher. No more heads are being taken. The enemy groups have become their friends. The members of the rising generation of Shapras are becoming full-fledged citizens of Peru and citizens of heaven.

They Saw a Great Light
<u>By Lorrie Anderson</u>

"...And thou shalt call His name <u>Jesus</u> for He shall save His people from their sins." (Matthew 1:21)

Four years ago, the Shapra Indians of northern Peru had never even heard the name of Jesus.

"...God so loved the world..." (John 3:16)

Three years ago, Doris Cox and I had arrived to live with them and learn their unwritten language. By Christmas we were just learning to converse and could not tell them the Christmas story. We could, however, tell them in simple terms of the loving heavenly Father who created them.

"For unto you is born this day in the city of David a Savior which is Christ the Lord." (Luke 2:11)

Last year I was able to translate the story of the birth of Christ with the help of Irina, the chief's wife. When the chief returned from a trip to the witchdoctor's, I checked it with him.

Doris was on furlough, but Rachel Saint was with me and we invited the Indians over for Christmas dinner. As we sat on the palm board floor of our thatched hut eating with our hands, it was a strange but enjoyable Christmas dinner.

"The people which sat in darkness saw great light; and to them which sat in the region and shadow of death, light is sprung up."
(Matthew 4:16)

This year I'm glad to be able to spend Christmas with my family but some of you prayed, so that for a few of the Shapras it will be a real Christmas—the first one with meaning, for what is Christmas without Christ Sin the heart? Just before I left there in March for furlough, I was able to finish translating the Gospel account of the death and resurrection of Christ.

In August Doris returned there, accompanied by Beth Hinson, a nurse—and besides working on language analysis and primers, she has been reading the translations over and over to them.

One day in September, after several days of drunken "fiesta" Tariri—realizing the hopelessness of life without Christ—came of his own accord to ask how he could receive Jesus as his Savior. The first Candoshi believer!

(Our Shapras, and the more distant Muratos, are all part of the same Candoshi tribe.) Later the same day his son, Tsirimpo, (about 12 or 13 years old) was also born again by faith in Christ. Since then, five others—Matarina, Tanchima, Sinora, Shimbotka, and young Shiniki—have said that they too believe and want to follow Jesus. But don't think that things will be easy now, for Satan won't give up even one of his subjects without a fight—for he has ruled there too long. So, we must pray!

What God did for the Piros and Cashibos, He is now doing for the Shapras. And do you know what broke through the barriers of tribal custom, witchcraft, and fear, with which Satan had bound them all? It was the hearing of the ***Word of God*** in their *own* languages!

"The entrance of Thy words giveth light. it giveth understanding unto the simple…" (Psalm 119:130)

Lorrie Doris Anderson, 1953

Chapter 11 - Importance of Radio Contact

Perhaps you'd be interested in the testimony Lorrie Anderson gave us recently of what the radio has meant to two single girls working with a savage tribe of Shapras.

"The time that Dottie Svendsen and I appreciated the radio the most was during the recent crisis, when several of our Indians were killed. It had been a quiet January day—quiet days are rare in Shapraland, and the children suddenly became excited. "Here's Shiniki's dog," they shouted as a wet bedraggled dog ran up the hill. Shiniki lives three days upstream, and we weren't expecting him, so it was a surprise. But everyone was happy to have him come, especially when they looked and saw three canoes, one with Mama and Maria. They hadn't been down to visit yet since I'd returned from furlough. But our joy soon turned to sadness, for Shiniki had not come for a visit, but they were running away from a scene of terrible bloodshed.

Shiniki's voice was high-pitched, and I could hardly understand him with everyone talking at once. Finally, when they got talked out, I told Shiniki that I wanted to tell my people by radio, so I needed to get the story straight. "Are Wautista and Tayanta really dead? Did you see them dead? They aren't just hurt?" "No, they were lying there dead. Sombra was only shot in the wrist, but he would surely bleed to death." Of course, I warned Doris immediately because I knew she would want to know, and because I wanted everyone at the base to pray with us (Doris is Lorrie's partner, who was doing some special language work at the base while Dottie Svendsen temporarily took her place in the tribe.) We went on the air and the base radio was on. I told them I had to talk to Doris right away, as soon as there was a lull in the busy schedule. They brought her to the radio right away without any questions. (I have been so thankful for the patience and understanding of the radio operators, not only at this time but all year around.)

I think perhaps it was the next day, or maybe a few days later, when old Shutka (the father of Wautista and Tayanta) was on the warpath, that Harold Goodall came to the radio and assured us that a plane was standing by if we should need to come out of the tribe, and that everyone at the base was praying for us. Oh, that was welcome news!

The last thing we wanted to do was to leave our Shapras, but it was good to know that JAARS (the Jungle Aviation and Radio Service) was standing by and that folks cared and were praying for us.

During the next two weeks we had a radio schedule every day—three or four times a day. Every day there were new developments, I wanted to tell Doris about people arriving who were running away from the vengeance of the upriver crowd, people leaving in the middle of the night, messages of new developments from upriver. Each day I was able to report to Doris at length. It was not only that the daily radio contact made us feel safe, but to be able to keep the folks at the base posted, and know they were following us with prayer, meant more that we can tell, for we were not afraid for ourselves, but we were concerned for our Indians (they were like family to us), and wanted you to pray with us for them. When the revenge party went breaking out threats against the runaway killers, it was wonderful to be able to ask you by radio to stand by us with prayer. We are sure the outcome would have been different had you not prayed and kept those bullets from hitting their mark and kept women and children from the violence that was threatened.

"It may not be so necessary in some tribes, but we felt that if it were not for JAARS and the radio contact, and the planes, we could not stay out there. It is because we have contact with the outside world that more violence has not been done."

In closing, I would like to give you one of the most logical and striking arguments ever spoken for Bible translation work. When Uncle Cam (Mr. Townsend) went to the Shapra tribe for a visit, he had several talks with Tariri, the converted chief. As they were parting, he urged Tariri to help our Wycliffe girls all he could so they could translate the Word of God into his language, and train Indians to teach the tribe to read the Scriptures. Chief Tariri's reply was:

"We will help them, how can we remember God's Word and live as He wants us to live, when it isn't written on paper for us to see? We hear it and understand, it enters our hearts; then we forget it. We keep forgetting what it says. If we had it on paper, we would do just as Uncle Cam has done for us (teaching and explaining the Word.) We could open it up and say, 'Now listen, it says this and this and this. And listen to this.' Just among ourselves we could do that. And we wouldn't forget it."

Chapter 12 - A Big Enough Chief

Richard Pittman
Chief Tariri of the Candoshi-Shapras in Peru proved to be a capable, versatile guide and teacher to both his own people and to SIL. He provided facilities for linguists, promotion of literacy, and improvement of living conditions in his area. He even participated in public programs in both Peru and the U.S.

"Tariri, are you a big enough chief to take care of my linguists, or will I need to send out an airplane?" asked a voice from a radio.

The director at Yarinacocha was checking on the safety of linguists Lorrie Anderson and Doris Cox during a dangerous day; a group of Candoshi-Shapras in northern Peru had gone on a drinking spree. The director, four hours away by plane, was calling by radio and asking to speak to Chief Tariri.

When Tariri heard that the big chief (general director of SIL) was going to speak to him by radio, he painted his face and put on all his headgear and decorations. Stepping up to the microphone, he answered, "I *am* a big enough chief. Don't you worry. I will take care of them."

Although Chief Tariri had given permission in 1950 for the linguists to live among the Shapras, everyone else objected. All the other Shapra men said, "You are a big chief—you have killed many people and you are our leader. Why are you allowing outsiders to come in and exploit us?"

He answered, "They are only women. They are probably just looking for husbands." He let them come; with keen propriety they called him brother. In the Shapras' culture a brother is obligated to take care of his sisters. Tariri let them stay even though some complained.

Faithfulness to his culture and an innate sense of leadership made Chief Tariri a protector of the two ladies living among the headhunters to learn the language and translate the New Testament for them.

Later there were incidents which showed the effect on Tariri of having listened to the teaching of these translators.

After receiving a defective outboard motor, Tariri dictated this letter to a Swedish merchant in Lima:

"You sent me a bad motor. You don't know me. Even though we are Shapras we don't like that sort of thing… I used to take off heads…"

The Candoshi-Shapras, like their distant Jivaro cousins, were skilled not only in headhunting but also in head shrinking. Tariri had done more than his share. A belt woven of hair from ten of his enemies had once adorned his waist.

"When people sent bad messages to us, we said, 'Because they want to die, they do that.' Then we went and killed them. We traveled far. We used to raid, take the women, and kill the young men. We told our young men and boys to kill so that when they grew up, they would not be afraid to kill. That is what I used to do before the girls came."

"Jesus overcame me," announced Tariri, concluding his letter to the Swedish merchant. "Even though I used to take off heads, I have quit doing so. Even though you sent me a bad motor, I love you."

Replacement parts for the motor were promptly dispatched!

Spitting the Truth
Lorrie Anderson, Ethel Wallis, and Thelma Johnston

"Oh, the floors were so beautiful; they were white. And I ate their food. I did not like it very much. I wanted to spit it out sometimes, but I'd look at that beautiful floor and think, where can I spit it? There was no place I could spit!" These were Chief Tariri's comments after his first visit to Lima and his stay in the SIL house there.

The Candoshi-Shapras have a custom of spitting as they talk. This proves they are telling the truth. Failure to spit indicates the speaker is lying; he must spit frequently.

Tariri took his responsibilities as chief seriously, even before he heard the Gospel. He had earned this position mainly by killing. The more killed, the greater the chief—and Tariri had killed many. People throughout the area looked up to him. He referred to himself as "Chief of Seven Rivers"; he could call on the men in all those areas to go on a raid and kill for revenge.

As a leader he had to be a good talker. Tariri is an orator, very intelligent, with a large vocabulary. "Chief Tariri uses words that we do not understand," said one of his bright young men.

A chief also had to be a hard worker, one who labored along with the men, just as hard as they, or harder. This was another quality which made Tariri a great chief.

"When Tariri returns, perhaps he and I can decide what to do," said Shutka, the upriver chief who, along with his five young sons, had been the terror of that part of the jungle. That Shutka would humble himself to acknowledge Tariri's better leadership was unheard of, and one more proof of Tariri's greatness.

What problem did Shutka want to discuss? One of his two wives and several of his children had died. Two sons, Wautista and Tayanta, were killed, perhaps by their brother-in-law in another upriver village. Shutka first threatened to kill every man, woman, and child in the village where the incident occurred. Many of the women and children fled downriver to the settlement where Lorrie Anderson and Dottie Svendsen were living.

Shutka and his part of six men followed some of their fleeing enemies to a distant river. There the old chief and one companion encountered the group. There was shooting at close range, but no one was hit. At this point Shutka decided to discuss the situation with Tariri.

Chief Tariri had not become a believer until he had spent an entire year pondering whether he could afford to follow the Gospel. Only one wife? No drinking? No witch doctoring? Worst of all, no killing!

As a believer Tariri remained a great chief, now a more compassionate one. When his first wife died before the linguists came, according to the custom he had not paid attention to her children lest his other wife, Irina, become jealous. Those children were left to sleep by the fire with no mosquito net. They made themselves a little tent out of bark cloth, too small; sometimes their feet stuck out and vampire bats bit their feet or noses and drank their blood. Tariri gave the children only enough food to keep them alive.

After he became a believer, Tariri took better care of the boys. He also fell in love with his wife Irina in a new way, and she with him. They were so much in love that he hated to go away and leave her behind. As he went off each day with the men to make a canoe, clear an area for a garden, hunt, or fish, he always said, "Now, Irina, I am going to go and I'll be back at…" He walked a little way, turned and said again, "Now I'll be back soon." He spoke again at the edge of the clearing—he could hardly tear himself away from her. Even his own people laughed!

Tariri helped Lorrie Anderson translate Bible stories. He loved those stories. They translated the stories when the day's work was done; the next day he would retell them to the men of the village as they worked together. The healing of the nobleman's son was his favorite. He always ended it: "and they never went to the shaman again!"

The biggest change came in Tariri's decision to stop killing. He had to face being called a coward and a traitor; he was threatened with:

"You are going to pay with your own skin if you will not lead us on a raid to kill our enemies!"

In his new zeal he attempted aggressive changes among his people. Part of their social life was drinking *masato,* a beer made from the long, starchy root of the manioc. One time, Tariri told all the women to dump out their big pots of *masato.* This was unfortunate because the people needed the vitamin B provided by the drink. If they had let it ferment only a little rather than become intoxicating, they could have had healthful results. Later, many developed this better approach.

The chief also once told them to get rid of all their tobacco plants. "Pull up your plants, root them up, and throw them away," he directed, "because tobacco is bad. We should not be using it to see visions." However, the people needed tobacco for medicinal use—to kill bot larvae which the fly had deposited under their skin as it bit them. Eventually they had to replant tobacco.

Tariri was always conscious of his appearance as chief. Sometimes he dressed in his "special occasions" outfit: a beautiful hand-woven poncho with tassels. Also, he put on beads, some made of seeds or bones; others were tiny glass kinds obtained from traders.

His colorful headdress was made from toucan tail feathers. The dozens of birds required to furnish the many small red and yellow feathers were never wasted—they added protein to the family diet. Long, iridescent green beetle wings were made into earrings.

When he was not wearing this outfit for a special occasion, he dressed in western-style shirt and pants. He then tied back his ponytail with rosettes of toucan feathers. If he later decided to visit someone important, he added the headdress, earrings, and perhaps some of his necklaces.

On the tenth anniversary of SIL in Peru, Tariri went to Lima for the celebration. He spoke frankly there, as he always did with his own people and with the linguists. He told his audiences that he gave up killing when he became a believer. He also said to them, "You people, I see, are smoking tobacco. You should not be doing that." Suddenly the cigarettes disappeared behind the backs of smokers or landed on the floor.

There were, of course, many adjustments for him to make in Lima; one was caused by claustrophobia. He was not used to solid doors and walls. Candoshi houses had either no walls, or merely siding of *pona* (palm board) with slits; usually they had no doors at all. The only privacy was mosquito netting made of heavy mousseline. In Lima he refused to completely close even the bathroom door!

When Ralph Edwards decided to feature Rachel Saint on his show, "This Is Your Life," he brought Tariri to California, because Rachel had spent a year in his village along with Lorrie Anderson. En route to the show, Tariri and Don Burns made a rest stop at a gas station. Don was waiting outside while Tariri was in the men's room—with the door ajar. When another man headed for the door, Don blocked his way and said, "Just a minute. There's an Indian chief in there."

The man looked around. "Is this 'Candid Camera?'" he asked.

When Chief Tariri walked out in his formal attire, the astonished traveler continued to look for the "candid camera"!

Tariri remains a great chief, worthy of any camera, and of the respect he has received in both the United States and Peru.

Chapter 13 - Chief Tariri

My first impression of Chief Tariri is sitting in his canoe watching him paddle the nine-hour trip up the Pushaga River to the community where Dorrie and I would spend so many years living with the Shapra tribe.

He was an impressive man although not tall. He was only about 5'8" tall, but one hardly noticed his stature because he was a strong and vigorous man, and a very forceful presence. He talked loudly and continually. Of course, Dorrie and I had no idea at this point what he was saying, but it was clear to us he spoke with authority and was very sure of himself. We would later understand he thought of himself as Chief of Seven Rivers, meaning he was powerful enough to gather warriors from these seven river communities for action against enemies. He was one of two chiefs in the area, the other being the upriver chief, Old Shutka, who was Tariri's cousin.

Tariri was a handsome man with long dark hair and the beautiful Indian skin of his people. On important occasions, he wore an impressive head dress of feathers, much as a king would wear a crown. Tariri was an important person, and he knew it. He was a proud man with good reason. He was intelligent, a hard worker, an eloquent and prolific speaker, and a fearsome fighter and killer. He had a reputation and was well respected and feared in the seven-river area over which he claimed dominion. Even Cameron Townsend himself was impressed when he visited the Shapra and met Chief Tariri.

Dorrie and I were initially not wise in dealing with Chief Tariri. Looking back, we were rude, and even stupid to challenge him. Once when we did not defer to him and disapproved of something he was doing, he became very very angry with us. He said, "If you were my sisters, I would chase you with a spear. I would probably not kill you, but you would be frightened that I might." Lesson learned.

The Shapra were an intelligent people. Whereas some surrounding tribes could only count to three, or so, the Shapra had a system for counting involving fingers and toes, and through this system could count to infinity in groups of twenty. As a group was completed, there was a clap. Then claps were counted. It was an ingenious system, and there was a word for every number. They also had a name for every constellation. Such intellectual aptitude is no doubt part of the reason Tariri was receptive to Victorino's suggestion that he send missionaries to teach the people to read and write and to teach them about God. Tariri understood that knowledge is power.

When Tariri accepted, Victorino was evidently confident enough in Tariri's word to suggest to Cameron Townsend that he send us to the Shapra as missionaries. Victorino had found the Shapra to be a noble people who lived by their own version of the Ten Commandments. Granted, they came from a long line of vengeful killers, but they did not lie, they did not steal, they did not cheat, and they did not commit adultery. Such sins were severely punished, so they did not happen often. Once Dorrie and I were missing a spool of thread, and we suspected a certain young girl of taking it. But we said nothing for fear of the consequences that would befall the suspect. Later we found the spool behind something in the house, and we were so glad we had said nothing.

The Shapra lived by a moral code that other tribes did not all have. War was war, but life in the community was well regulated. So, when Tariri gave his word he would accept and protect us, his word was law. Even though many around us were suspicious of us as outsiders who would bring them harm, Tariri would not allow them to kill us. He often reminded the people of his responsibility to protect us. We learned to refer to him as our brother, and he called us his sisters. That made us part of his family over which he had responsibility. Our house was built in his clearing close to his own. He was kind to us and protected us. We were not completely aware at the time how much our lives depended on Chief Tariri.

Neither were we aware when we first arrived that we had come to live among notorious killers who came from generations of headhunters. Somehow it escaped Victorino's memory to tell us this detail. And indeed, we never saw a head shrinking nor saw an ornamental head hanging in a hut as decoration, formerly a common practice. The heads were considered quite beautiful. Tariri had a belt woven from the hair of some of his victims, but he did not wear it often in our presence. Perhaps Victorino had forewarned Tariri that we would not approve and might even be scared away by such tactics. We soon learned about the raids and the killings, however, and we lived in fear that our tribe would be attacked by another group seeking vengeance. This was a way of life in the Peruvian jungle before the people knew Christ. Only with much time and patience and God's help were we able to make changes to this way of life. Tariri would later become one of the strongest and most influential Christians in the area. Praise God for His power and mercy and goodness.

Tariri wants to be the Greatest Chief

"I wanted to be the greatest chief in the whole world. I wanted everyone to be afraid of me, so I lived from one war raid to the next. We made many gardens where we could hide out after a raid. We would creep up on a home, turn over their *masato* (yucca beer) pots and start killing the people. Then we would burn the house down and run away to one of the gardens we had made. The relatives of the dead people would look and look for us, but they never found us. If we knew they were getting close, we would go to another garden far away. Then when things had died down, we would go to another house and kill. That is how we were living when the English-speaking girls came to live with us."

"They didn't speak our language and it was hard to know what they were trying to say. They told us not to get drunk and not to kill. I wondered, 'Why do they say that?' But I didn't understand."

"Some of the men kept coming to me saying, Let's kill these English-speaking girls. Why are they here? No one speaking English has ever come here before. We have axes and machetes so let's kill them.'' But I said, 'No, not yet. **They have a message for us from Apanchi, and I want to know what it is**.' So finally, they said, 'Well, you are the chief,' and they stopped talking about killing them."

"Then, as the girls learned to speak more and more of our language, they told us more and more of the message from Apanchi, and I believed it and Apanchi changed my heart. Now I don't want to kill, not even a little bit."

"Brother Ngochima (John Tuggy) got us a lot of land from the government and now we make large gardens. I have lots of food. I even have oranges and lemons and we have cattle."

"Everyone should know God's Word. God sent Jesus so that He can forgive all the wicked things we did. Now we can live the way He wants us to live and not live killing people."

Tariri's Testimony

"I used to drink fermented drink and got drunk. We went far on a trail and killed people to take heads."

"That's the way we used to do. Before you people came, that's the way we did. Then I heard about Jesus. They told me about God, [the Father]. They told us His Word. How can I keep on killing if I believe these things, I thought? Even though I used to be like that, before I came to know God, after I received Jesus, then I left those things behind. Jesus overcame me. My heart went "wing" [zing] with joy."

"People say to me, 'Why don't you talk about killing anymore? Why have you, a powerful chief, stopped killing? Why do you just talk about Jesus?'"

"'Now listen to me with your ears,' I said. 'You should do the same,' I told them. 'Live well. Let's love only Jesus. Let's have His understanding. Why should we live bad, and get drunk, and kill, and hate? For our sins Jesus suffered and died to pay our debt. Why shouldn't we trust God? God gave the beautiful stars and moon to see by night. God lives on high. That's why I love to talk to God.'"

"Send people everywhere to teach about Jesus. Send lots of people to all the places where Jesus isn't known. Teach everyone—especially those who don't know. Send them to teach the love of Jesus, to those who live in ignorance."

Chapter 14 - Lorrie Shudders

Chief Tariri*
By Robert Griffin

Lorrie and Dorrie (as they are known to all of their friends) were the first white people to live among the head shrinking Candoshi Shapra. These young Americans went to Peru's northern jungle with one purpose: to learn the Shapra's language, design an alphabet, teach the people to master the mysteries of the "paper that talks" and translate at least the New Testament for them. They, and nearly 6000 others like them, according to Clarence W. Hall, belong to one of the most determined and effective groups now waging war on world illiteracy: the Summer Institute of Linguistics and its sister organization, the Wycliffe Bible Translators. JAARS, the technical support arm for the translation ministry, helps make the work possible in some of the most remote corners of the world. Currently working among almost 1200 language groups in 53 countries**, the translators encounter some unusual obstacles most every time they set out to analyze an unwritten language and prepare a Bible translation for a people for the very first time.

Earlier, when the JAARS airplanes first carried Lorrie and Dorrie to the Shapra people, Tariri was a proud and successful headhunter who maintained his position as chief by killing the tribal enemies. It puzzled the notorious killer that these two white girls wanted to come and live among them, but he permitted it, against strong opposition from everyone throughout his jungle domain.

"What harm can they do?" he asked. "They are only women. They are probably looking for husbands." Later he told Lorrie he felt they would somehow bring progress to his people. "He didn't know it," she adds, "but God was already working in his heart."

She says that once that he gave his permission, it was settled. His word was law. The Shapra men weren't enthused, but they accepted his decision. However, a major problem for Lorrie and Dori remained: the other women's hostility. It wasn't until they were both laid out with malaria, and the oldest lady of the village came to give grudging help, that they learned the reason.

"She told us they all looked on us as threats, as rivals," recalls Lorrie. The old lady instructed them to call the men "brothers". Once the tribal women knew the Americans were acknowledging their husbands as brothers, not potential husbands, the air cleared. Tariri told his people, "These women are our sisters. We must take care of them."

We were so green when we first stepped out on the beach," adds Lorrie. "We didn't know a word of Shapra, and they didn't know any Spanish, so we had to start from scratch using the monolingual approach. We were trained as linguists to do that, but we made lots of blunders. God blessed us, in spite of it. It was one of the happiest days of my life when, three years later, Chief Tariri gave his heart to the Lord, the first Shapra to believe. It was Dorrie's privilege to lead him to the Lord while I was on furlough."

Tariri didn't make a rash decision. For nearly 2 years he had been pondering the implications of the Gospel on his life and those of his people. When Tariri heard the first verse of Scripture to be translated into his language, he told the women, "When you talk like that, my heart leaps with understanding." But he knew a change of allegiance might cost him his life. He had already been threatened by the other warriors for not going with them on revenge-killing raids.

The old ways still pulled on Tariri. Could he believe the stories he was hearing about Jesus? Tariri had been taught from childhood that he had to kill to keep from being killed. "If people try to kill you, you kill back." That was the law of the jungle. Now Tariri wanted to live by another law. "What shall I do?" he asked himself, "shall I leave killing? Shall I stop fighting? If I leave fighting, people will think I am not a chief anymore." Then I thought, "What am I saying?" After a while, I thought, "That is what I will do, I will love God."

The neighboring Huambisa people, who had often felt the keen edge of the Shapra's revenge, couldn't understand the change. "What is wrong with Tariri?" they asked. "He doesn't go killing anymore."

"That's right," Tariri said, "God says not to kill. He has given me another heart. I love Jesus. Why would I think of killing?"

Once he had made the decision to follow Christ, Tariri threw himself into the translation effort. He spent hours with the translators, hours away from other duties, hours he could ill afford. But he was driven by enthusiasm as he saw his people being transformed from shameful killers to people who let "Jesus cleanse their hearts and help them live well."

"It was exciting for us too, and fulfilling, but it wasn't easy," Lorrie remembers.

"There were so many times I wanted to give up. I got cerebral malaria when I first went out to the Shapras and had an attack every two months for the first 18 years, in spite of taking the prophylactic medicines. That was tough, we couldn't have stayed out there without the regular service from JAARS planes and that prized electronic lifeline, our two-way radio. Our only source of supplies and help was 500 miles away with nothing between us and the translation center but pathless jungle. How we praise God for radios and airplanes, and for all the dedicated fellows who made them work!"

Lorrie says, people often ask: "How did you stand all the bugs and snakes, the heat, and malaria for all those years?" The tribe of headhunters among whom Lorrie and her Bible translation partner, Doris Cox, lived had warned the young women about the monster snakes—how the huge boas seized their prey and then quickly coil around the hapless creature, squeezing out breath, and life.

Her response is quick. "Those were minor annoyances—but there were worse. We, like the Shapra, lived in constant fear from the threats of their enemies. We endured the heartbreak of seeing Shapras killed in revenge killings of their own people. We grieved with them over the loss of loved ones, and struggled with them in their family problems. But the worst was the battle with the powers of darkness. It wasn't easy, and apart from the power of God working through us, we couldn't have stuck it out. But every bit of the trauma was worth it. Being able to give them God's Word written in their own language, and seeing the changes the Gospel brought to Shapra lives has made it more than worthwhile." says Lorrie. "I'd do it again if I could."

Chief Tariri's only regret is that it took so long for the missionaries to come. "If you had told us long ago, the old ones would have known it, too. Nevertheless, we praise God. Before you came, all was darkness. Now there is light."

Footnotes

* Chief Tariri was chief of the Shapra branch of the Candoshi tribe. He called himself, "Chief of Seven Rivers." He lived on the Pushaga River, at the headwaters of the Amazon River in the jungles of Peru, South America. In July 1950, two young American women went to live with the headhunting Shapra Indians to learn their language, and translate the Bible for them. The printed New Testament was distributed among them in April of 1980. Since they were completely monolingual, that is, spoke only their own language, they were in constant turmoil with their enemies, and were a hundred miles from any medical facilities, there were many distractions that kept them from making progress, and completing the translation.

** This article was written in 1989, so the statistics are not up to date. According to the latest statistics (2021), Wycliffe Bible Translators have given the New Testament, translated into their own heart language, to 717 language groups. We are currently working in 1582 languages from 70 different countries around the world.

There are 7378 different languages in the world. Of those, 3883 language groups still do not have even one word of the Bible in their language. They still need to have translators come to learn their language, and translate God's Word for them.

Chapter 15 - Chief Tariri Escapes Death One More Time

By Lorrie Anderson
February 8, 2016

Remember old Uncle Shutka? We had hoped this year might hold more happiness for him than the past, but I'm afraid it has been the unhappiest of his life.

Some of you know how earlier this year his two older sons were killed to retaliate for their killing of the witchdoctor, Sinta. Wautista, the older, was the darling of his community, and the apple of his mother's eye. Tayanta (remember his visit after Christmas last year?) was well-loved too. As terrible as this was to them, we hoped it would sober them up and make them realize that they can't go on killing, and expect to escape being killed off themselves. When Shutka and remaining sons followed the killers through the jungle and were prevented in a miraculous way from hitting them, though they shot at close range, I think Shutka and Pinchu at least were willing to "Call it quits".

Although he is not a believer, old Shutka seemed tired of a life of killing and said, "*Wapa!* (that's enough!) God must have kept us from killing them. If we don't stop, all my children will be killed." I believe he meant it, but Inchi, his wife, was not satisfied. She has kept after them to kill, kill, kill! When Chief Tariri invited them down (or is "ordered" the word?) to talk and receive the machetes the Ministry of Education sent, Inchi begged them not to go. "Tariri is just lying. He wants to get you all down there and kill you," she said. But they didn't think so, and came anyway.

Now the saddest news of all comes to us by two-way radio. Doris and I left Pushaga early last month—she to attend a linguistic workshop with Dr. Pike, and I to be with Jeanne Grover among the Aguarunas, since her partner Mille was also invited to attend, on October 15.

Here is how it happened: Early the previous morning Chiriapa, Irina's brother, arrived at Tariri's house to work with him in his chacra. Young Shiniki, Tariri's younger brother, had come too. They were surprised by a visit from Shutka and sons. Though they hadn't blown their "horn" as the canoe drew near, Chief Tariri, suspecting nothing, invited them to sit down. In a split second he realized it was not a friendly visit as Pirocha, one of Tariri's sons, stood pointing his gun at him. "Don't shoot me," Tariri said, "I don't want to kill you, why do you want to kill me?" Pirocha shot and the bullet entered Tariri's chest, piercing the lung and going out the shoulder. (The doctor later said that the bullet was only ¼ inch from his heart.) "I felt my heart go *shte* and I felt faint, and blood gushed out," he said.

Then Pinchu shot Chiriapa. His sister, Arosa, threw herself on Chiriapa shouting to her father and brothers, "Don't kill my husband!" As she did so, the baby on her back was shot through the head by a bullet intended for her husband. Dear baby Toripi—he was my favorite baby boy—so sweet and happy. Old Shutka aimed at Tariri twice and his gun just went click, click, and the third time the bullet missed him. At the same time Pirocha aimed and shot, and again the bullet whizzed by his other ear. (*For He will give His angels charge of you to guard you in all your ways.* Psa. 91:11.) As soon as the shooting had started Irina, Tariri's wife, with a baby on her back, and one in her arms, ran off. The other children ran, and hid also. Teenagers Shiniki, and Tsirimpo, (Tariri's son) ran into the gardens, and sat there trembling, and praying for God's protection over Chief Tariri.

Tariri managed to wrest the gun from Shutka's hands, and ran for his life. It was the only sensible thing to do—five against one and all armed. I'm sure it was the first time in his life he ever ran from anyone, or anything. A few years back I think Tariri would have stayed and fought all five, even if it meant losing his own life. He would have had the glory of dying fighting. Now, rather than killing and being killed, he wants to live and point others to the Way of Life.

That's what he tried to do when Shutka and sons came down on those two previous visits. He witnessed to them at length of what Christ did for us in His death and what He had done in His life. "Let's all live together in peace now. Let's leave fighting and killing," he said. He even invited them to come down and live closer so they could all live happily together. Chief Tariri said, "Look I have no gun in my hands— only the Word of God," (actually, a little Wordless Book with colored pages to remind him of the story. How I wish we did have the Word of God printed in their language.) No Shapra man ever goes visiting, or entertains, without a gun, or spear, in his hands.

Why did they come to kill? I don't know what exact reason they'd give. It was probably connected with their sons' deaths—Chiriapa was related to those who killed them. Since they couldn't get the actual killers, they finally went after him—even though he was their brother-in-law.

Our little plane flew 300 or 400 miles and took Chief Tariri back to our base, where he could be under the doctor's care. He is improving but is still weak. He'll be returning to his family at the same time we do in a few days. They have abandoned houses, and fields, up on the Pushaga so we will all be living on a small lake in temporary shelters for a while.

Oh, what heartache when we heard the news. Not only for Chiriapa and his baby, who were killed, but for those who killed them, and tried to kill Tariri. It hurt because I'd trusted them. But they felt they had a legitimate reason, no doubt. They believed that no man dies a natural death. He is either killed by another man or bewitched by a witchdoctor who sends "magical darts" which cause sickness. So, every death must be avenged. The people of our area, whom we have been able to treat with medicine over a number of years, have been convinced that at least some deaths are caused by sickness apart from witchcraft. The upriver crowd has not learned this, and keeps on with their revenge. If they keep on, soon there will be no men left there. This saddens us, for we love them as much as those among whom we live. Humanly speaking we will never see them again. But with Abraham, we look not at the facts as they appear to us. *Abraham looked at the facts… yet he refused to allow any distrust… to make him waver. He remained absolutely convinced that God was able to implement His own promise.* Romans 4:20, 21 (Phillips).

Lorrie Anderson, November 1955

Chapter 16 - Point Blank

by Chief Tariri, translated by Lorrie Anderson

I, Tariri, Chief of Seven Rivers, set forth this truthful declaration:

The sky was overcast. There was a chill in the air, and an ominous rumble of thunder from the darkening clouds. Why did I feel it was a portent of disaster? I shook my head to throw off such thoughts.

I had looked forward to today. I had invited *Sirikima** (brother-in-law) Chiriapa over to help me clear a patch of woods for a new chacra. I wanted to plant lots of peanuts and manioc.

I enjoyed working with *Sirikima*—quiet, shy, congenial. I thought about this serious-faced brother of Irina's—tall, lanky, far from handsome, with his straight black hair hanging to his shoulders. He would probably come for work without a shirt because he owned only one. His oldest skirt, a handwoven wrap-around, would be faded, stained, and ragged along the edge. He would have his machete in one hand, his spear in the other. This he would jab hard into the ground nearby, handle end down, before he sat down. His arrival interrupted my revere. He greeted me, "*Tamarimta, tarish, Sirikima*? (How are you? Are you here, brother-in-law?)"

"*Aa, tartana* (Yes, I am here)," I answered, "*Kchinanki, kchinanki!* (Have a seat, have a seat!)"

He sat on the palm board platform, comfortable, but not relaxed. Irina was at our side before I got the words out of my mouth, "Irina, serve your brother *kapóssi.*"

How Irina loved this brother of hers! He was her favorite, a gentle giant, a man of peace. As is our custom, there was no communication between them, not even a greeting, not a smile. She kept filling the drinking gourd with the fermented *manioc* drink until her brother had his fill and said, "*waapa.*"

Then she served me again before she went to the back of the hut to serve *kapóssi* to her brother's wife, Arosa, who had entered unobtrusively. Her baby boy, bouncing up and down in the sling on her back, making happy, gurgling sounds, laughed out loud. We paid no attention to the women, but turned away to talk of our plans.

It was about 6:00 am. *Sirikima* had come early to help me get a good start, as we Shapras like to do. He is not a joker, constantly laughing and teasing, like most Shapra men, but he feels comfortable around me.

After a little good-natured bantering my spirits lifted, and I forgot my dark thoughts. I liked this man. We had a good relationship. I loved him like a brother.

"Let's get going," I said—but with the very utterance of my words came the sound of a cow's horn. "Po-o, po-o, po-o," it said. "Who could that be? I'm not expecting anyone," I said. "Well, I suppose it could be your father-in-law, Old Shutka." He had said they would come back when they had more animal skins to trade. But I did not expect them this soon.

I turned around and looked toward the river. Sure enough, here they came, four of them, around the bend upriver. They were not paddling; they were just floating along in a leisurely manner. They seemed in no hurry. There was just one wild boar's skin in the bottom of the canoe, rolled up and tied. "That's strange," I thought, but before I had time to consider this, they were at the shore.

I was naïve and trusting. The signs were all there that they had not come to socialize, but my mind rejected that. The suspicion lingered, but I pushed it down into my subconscious. This was my relative, my cousin. Why should I fear him?

Irina was more discerning, less ready to trust. As they started walking slowly up the hill, she ran out to me and said, "They may be deceiving you. Maybe they are coming to kill you."

"Why would my father's relative want to kill me?" I said. "In any case, God will protect me."

But I had second thoughts. "What if they do intend to kill me?" I thought. So, I loaded my shotgun. I blushed to think I might be afraid. I, the great Tariri, who feared no one and nothing, but who was feared by everyone. What had I become? Afraid of my own cousin, no less! (I smile to recall it now.) I took the shells out of my gun, slipped them in my pocket, and laid down my gun. Then I sat down again on the platform and waited for them to reach the house.

Sirikima was standing behind me. He seemed nervous. His younger brother had recently taken part in the killing of Old Shutka's two favorite sons, Wautista and Tayanta, it was said. The brother denied it, but that's what some of the upriver people said. Revenge was called for. Even though their custom allowed a relative to be killed in place of the one who actually took part in the killing, *Sirikima* had not expected to be the object of their retaliation. He was sure they would be kind to the husband of their daughter and sister. They seemed to like him. Everyone liked him. He had no enemies. He was a man of peace.

Sirikima's beautiful young second wife, Arosa, hurried to him. She carried their handsome baby on her back, a large gourd in her hand. "I'm going to the river to get water," she said, and ran down the hill to meet her father and brothers.

By the time they reached the top of the hill, Arosa had got the water and was walking up behind her father.

Old Shutka's sons, Pirocha and Pinchu, came up to me first and said, "*Tamarimta, tarish, Ichia?* (How are you? Are you here, Uncle)?"

"*Tartana, tartana* (I am here, I am here)," I answered. "*Pshtogi, zowaa* (come in, brother)," I said to their father. "*Kchinanki, kchinanki.*"

I noticed they were agitated. Their eyes shone with anticipation.

I shooed my little boy away. "Go outside," I said.

They did not sit down. In a split second I realized that it was not a friendly visit as Pirocha stood staring at me, his eyes as hard as the steel of the Winchester he was holding. Suddenly he pointed his rifle at me.

"Don't shoot me," I said. "I don't want to kill you. Why do you want to kill me? I am unarmed. I don't even have a gun in my hands."

When I said that, they all pointed their rifles at us—two facing me, Old Shutka and Pirocha; two more, Pinchu and another young warrior, facing *Sirikima.* Unarmed, *Sirikima* grabbed for their guns and all three of them tussled together.

They overcame him, and once again trained their guns on us. They pulled the triggers on their rifles, but they just clicked. They were shooting point blank at me, but the bullets did not explode. God protected me. It was like a dream. It seemed like everything was in slow motion. They pointed their rifles at me again, saying, "*Ch-ch-cha!*"

I should have been terrified, but I was too stunned to be afraid. I was unbelieving. Why was this happening? I had told them about God. They listened. I thought they were beginning to believe. Old Shutka was my father's beloved cousin! His son, Pirocha, had married Chiriapa's and Irina's beautiful sister, Tsimari. She was the prize that many of the men, young and old, had sought. Pirocha had won. He and Tsimari had a new baby boy. He should be rejoicing at his good fortune, I thought. He should be at home hunting and fishing and caring for them—not out for revenge, killing people who had nothing to do with the killing of his brothers. I was filled with grief, as much for them as for me, as I thought of the great gap that yawned between us.

Pirocha—friend, foe, brother, cousin—what was he? Certainly, the latter, a cousin I called "brother"—son of my father's beloved cousin. But foe? Rival, yes. He won the prize—the most sought after Shapra girl, and the most beautiful.

Tsimari, Irina's sister, the one I wanted for my second wife. I'd asked for her, but her brother, Chiriapa, refused.

Shapra girls seldom—almost never—have a choice, but Tsimari wanted to marry only a young, single man. She didn't want to be a co-wife, not even with her loving sister, Irina. And kindly Chiriapa, who loved her dearly, deferred to her wishes.

I was angry, but God overcame me. Maybe we couldn't be close friends, but I thought we could at least engage in the trade of animal skins and *goma* [the sticky sap of a tree used in making waterproof duffle bags, glue, and such.] We had done a little trading, and I had begun telling him about the Lord, along with his father and brothers.

Now Pirocha stood pointing his rifle at me. The picture of his standing there like that is etched upon my mind forever.

His black hair, slightly wavy, hung halfway down his back. He was handsome, I must admit. The *kamasina* (young unmarried women) said he was "gorgeous, like an *arovi* (a lovely little black jungle bird with markings of red, blue, and green)." This to them is the epitome of beauty.

He was dressed with a new black and white striped skirt, hand-woven for him by his mother, topped by a pure white poncho hanging loose with fringe at the bottom. The skirt was held up by a colorful hand-woven belt. His feet were bare.

He had on a simple seed necklace. He did not have feather ornaments on his head, nor had he painted his face with *achiote* (paprika) in designs to make him look fierce as we do when we go on a killing raid. The element of surprise was a factor. He looked like he was going on a visit.

His purpose was evident now. But why? Pirocha stared at me, his eyes as hard as the steel of his Winchester. His face was now contorted with anger (whipped up in recent days by his mother's constant ravings for revenge, I was told later.) His gun was cocked. His muscles were tense.

They seemed possessed. Pirocha kept his rifle trained on me. His handsome face, with the long black slightly wavy hair hanging down, was contorted. Our eyes met. His were hostile. He had closed his heart to me, as had his father who, by his own confession, once loved me.

Pirocha gripped his Winchester rifle hard, his muscles tensed. There was fear in his eyes now, fear and excitement, a kind of exhilaration. I thought I saw his hands shake, but it was almost imperceptible.

He pulled the trigger again. I turned sideways to avoid the bullet, but to no avail. It entered my chest, piercing my lung, and going out my shoulder. I felt my heart go *shteyee!* Blood gushed out of the hole in my chest.

About the same time young Pinchu shot at *Sirikima* Chiriapa, his brother-in-law, and mine.

His sister, Arosa, threw herself on Chiriapa shouting, "Don't kill my husband!" As she did so, the bullet intended for her husband entered the head of the baby on her back, their beloved Toripi, killing him instantly.

Pinchu shot again, this time killing *Sirikima*. The keening death wail could be heard all over the jungle as Arosa cried and chanted, "*Zaranchinaa, zaranchinaa! Ipaarinaa, ipaarinaa!* (My husband, my husband! My baby, my baby!)" It is an all-enveloping cry that stabs one's heart—but it was my own grief for Chiriapa that pierced my heart with a pain that rivaled the bullet wound in my chest.

I managed to wrest the gun from Shutka's hands, and then I ran for my life. It was the only sensible thing to do. There were too many of them, and they were all armed. That's the first time in my life that I ran away from anyone or anything.

A few years ago, I would have stood my ground and fought to the death. To me, fighting, killing, and even being killed was glorious—so long as I died fighting. Now, rather than killing and being killed, I want to live and point others to the Way of Life.

That is what I had tried to do when Old Shutka and his sons came down on the two previous visits. I told them all I knew of Jesus—His birth, His life, His death, what it meant to us, and what Jesus had done in *my* life. I had said, "Let us all live together in peace. Let us leave all fighting and killing." I had even invited them to come downriver and live closer, so we could all live happily together. I had said, "Look, I have no gun in my hand—only God's Word."**

The crack of a twig brought me back to reality. Pirocha was following me. I could hear footsteps behind me. I kept running, but at the edge of the clearing I fell. My heart went *tum!* I was so weak from the loss of blood. Blood was gushing from my nose. I was vomiting blood. Then I got a burst of energy, as if God just lifted me up and stood me on my feet again. I made another dash with the strength He gave me.

Just then Pirocha turned back. God sent him back the way he came. I think God spooked him and struck fear into his heart. Pirocha knew I had his father's gun. I did not have time to load it, but he did not think of that, perhaps. He must have thought, Tariri is lying in ambush, waiting to shoot me when I appear. God is good. He took care of me.

I ran and ran until I came to Tanchima's clearing. I said, "Shutka shot me," even though it was Pirocha's bullet which hurt me. Shutka had shot again and again at point-blank range, but the gun did not discharge its bullets.

"Why would my own relative shoot me?" I asked.

I could not breathe. I moaned and gasped for breath. Strange noises came from my lungs. "Father, help me," I cried. I did not forget to pray and ask God's help even then.

I ran farther, and came to the house of my brother, Tsowinki. "Take me down to Soplin's for medicine," I said. "Surely they have something to help me." Soplin was the *patrón* with whom we traded, and for whom we worked occasionally.

I remember seeing the newly picked cotton piled up in his house. I was crying and moaning, in great pain. He gave me camphor to drink. They rubbed some kind of ointment on me also. I felt a little better, but was still hemorrhaging. Brother Tsowinki sent a runner to the Huambisas, young Antonio, who could speak their language. He was to inform Chief Wanka of my plight, and also to have David Beasley, the linguist there, call Yarinacocha by radio and ask for a plane to come to get me, and take me there. I hoped that the doctor there, with God's help, could save my life.

David sent word to Mpawachi (Doris Cox), at Yarinacocha, that I had been shot. After consulting with the big Chief there as to how it could be paid for and when a plane would be available, arrangements were made for an emergency flight right away.

My old friend and brother, Don Smith, was the pilot. Sister Miika (Mary Beth Hinson), a nurse, accompanied him to care for me and attend to my needs on the flight. Sister Mpawachi came along too, to make sure everyone understood one another. It made my heart happy to see them. It gave me hope that I might live. I surely would have died if left out there.

The sun was just setting when I arrived at the mouth of the Pushaga with my brother Tsowinki who had paddled hard since mid-morning to get me there.

We took off in the small hydroplane at the first light of dawn the next day. I was only half-conscious as we flew, but I noticed after a while that the motor hesitated. It seemed okay, but then it hesitated again.

Brother Don suddenly became very busy with all the little knobs on the panel of the plane and other things overhead and on the floor, but he did not appear worried. He was calm.

Brother Don shouted into the microphone, and someone shouted back. Then it was very quiet as he continued to pull and push a little knob. As he did, the motor coughed, then roared like one howl of a jaguar, and died.

I became more alert. I looked out of the window of the small plane. There was nothing but jungle as far as I could see. There were no rivers in sight. There was no place to land. The plane was just gliding down, down, slowly. The silence was terrifying. My heart beat faster. I could not see Sister Miika's face. She was up front next to the pilot. Sister Mpawachi was next to me, her face pressed against the other window. "*Pantsachpariniya* (We'll surely crash)," I said to myself. I called out silently, "*Apaa, istaantaa. Aapiyonaa. Potankcha, pantsatoronepa* (Father, help me. Take hold of the plane. Don't let us fall)."

It seemed a long time as we continued to drift down. Brother Don kept pumping the big knob. Suddenly the engine caught again, and again, and finally roared. Then it started to purr like a great big, contented jaguar. I lay back. Just like that a great peace came to me.

Sister Miika said later that Brother Don told her what had happened. As we were flying the crossover—a stretch between two rivers where the float plane had no place to land—the engine sputtered and died. He tried everything possible to start it as the plane began losing altitude. Nothing seemed to work. He prayed, and kept pumping the throttle. Finally, just as he thought we would surely crash into the top of the trees, the engine started again. We had glided almost to the other river at the end of the crossover. Brother Don had thought if he could make it to the river, he could make a forced landing there.

To this day, Brother Don does not know why the engine cut out. Perhaps a speck of dirt had gotten into the gas line. I have no doubt in my mind that Satan was trying one more way to destroy me. He had tried many times before to kill me. I know it was God who kept us from crashing in the jungle. Even if we had somehow survived the crash, I do not see how we could have gotten out of that jungle. What we were flying over is a wide, wide *aguaje* swamp—no solid land at all. You can see the sun shining on the water between the palm trees as you fly over. There are anacondas, and boas, and poisonous snakes there, as well as other wild creatures. God spared my life once again. That is why I say that God is great!

Chapter 17 - Tariri Forgives His Enemies

Chief of Seven Rivers Once Again Bows Before Greatest Chief

by Lori Anderson.

"Monchanki [that's my Shapra Indian name], why am I not getting better? Before I started swelling up and lately finding it hard to breathe, I was fine. There's nothing wrong with my heart. I was going off alone in my canoe to fish on the big river where the current is strong. I worked hard with my machete all day in the *chacra*."

"Brother Tariri, two different doctors have said that your old heart is enlarged, and the muscles are flabby. It just can't pump the blood well anymore (he had congestive heart failure.) They say there is nothing they can do for you anymore."

"Then why doesn't God heal me?" Tariri asked. Gracie said to me, "Tell him, maybe there are some people he needs to forgive." I did. I told him and explained that whether God chooses to heal him miraculously, or chooses to take him to Heaven, this was something he had to deal directly with God Himself. "Yes, there are," he said, and named a number of people, among them Basha and family, still in exile as a result of their killing of Oroshpa, Tariri's son.

This was a tough one. Could Tariri forgive them? He'd held that bitterness in his heart for many years. Yes, he would, he said, he'd tell the Lord. He made a list with those person's names, and prayed through the whole list, forgiving them. When he'd finished his face was radiant. As we continued to speak with him, he burst into a spontaneous song of praise, making up the words as he went along!

If God had not helped me, I would have died. The doctor took good care of me at Yarinacocha, and when I was well, they flew me back out to Pucacuro, on the big Morona River, the temporary camp my brother had set up for his family and mine until we could find a good place to settle permanently.

I was sad to leave my home on the Pushaga river, where we lived for so many years. There, Irina and I had made our home, and raised our older children. My big, recently built house with the oval thatched roof, so beautifully woven of the *yarinchi* palm was there. My large *chacra* with many crops, my hunting grounds with abundant game, and the small river with all the fish we could catch and eat. All that work for nothing. We had to begin over again. But all that was nothing compared to the loss of Irina's brother, dear *Sirikima*. We mourned him for a long time. Irina has never stopped grieving for him.

How could I forgive Old Shutka, and Pirocha, and the others for killing *Sirikima*, and trying to kill me? I could not. I was very angry. I wanted to kill all the upriver people. I wanted to wipe them out. I had tried in every way to make peace with them. I had encouraged them to stop killing and live in peace with everyone. This was their answer.

I heard much later that Shutka and Pinchu had already decided they had better stop killing before they and their extended family were finished off themselves. But Shutka's wife, Inchi, kept nag-nag-nagging, and demanding the death of someone in revenge for the death of her much-loved sons, Wautista and Tayaanta.

It is hard for a man to resist the taunts: "What kind of man are you? No man at all! How can you fail to uphold the honor of our family by not getting revenge?" The piercing death wail, day after day for months on end, wears a person down. No wonder the killing goes on and on!

But I did not think that way at first. I only wanted to kill in turn. That is what I did in the old days. If people wronged me, I killed them. This time I also wanted revenge. Some of my own people kept after me to seek revenge. They taunted me. "What kind of chief are you? You are a fake. If you do not go and kill our enemies, you are no chief. You will pay for it with your own skin."

I was in a turmoil. Besides the physical weakness and the pain as I was recovering, there was the constant criticism wearing me down. It made me very angry.

We had no contact with Old Chief Shutka and his sons for many years. Actually, he died before we saw them again. That made me sad. In the meantime, however, an old witchdoctor and a young man from their community strayed into our territory. We captured them and the soldiers downstream gave us permission to keep them in custody for a while as hostages. They were terrified and sure we would kill them. Instead, we kept them with us, and treated them well. We gave them plenty to eat. They stayed with us for several months. Every day I taught them from God's Word. I finally took pity on old Tsowinki's wife and children, who needed him, and sent them home. Kambosoro, the young one, was still single.

I told them once again what I had been telling them every day while they were here—that the only reason I was not killing them was because I loved God now, and no longer wanted to kill. They said, "Thank you,

thank you, Tariri; now we know it is really true that you love God."
(But that is another long story which I have already told to brother
Gochima [John Tuggy] on tape, and he put it in a book about me.
[**Tariri, My Story** by Ethel Wallis, Harper and Row, now out of print.])

I could not believe it myself—the change in me. I really was a
different person. That is why I say, "God overcame me. He overcame
my anger. He helped me forgive my enemies." Even when I got well
and strong again, I did not go to seek revenge on them. I did not seek to
kill old Chief Shutka and his sons. "Let them live and grow old with
their wives and children," I said. "Let them die in peace." This was not
me. I was the same old Tariri, in the same old body, but I had a *new*
heart. God had changed me from a killer to a man who loves his
enemies and wants them to know God also. That is why I say, "God is
great."

*The term "brother" is used for all close male relatives.

**Actually, the Word was not in print in Shapra at that point. What he
had was the little Wordless Book with colored pages to remind him of
the key points of the way of salvation. This was very significant because
no Shapra or Candoshi goes anywhere, nor entertains visitors in his
home, without a spear or gun in his hand.

Chapter 18 - Chief Tariri's Testimony

Chief Tariri – Shapra-Candoshi

by Tariri. Translated by Lori Anderson.

I used to kill people all the time. I was the greatest chief there. I lived very bad. Men came from far away to talk to me about killing. They said, "Tariri isn't afraid to go kill our enemies." We became famous for our killing. We used to drink *kapóssí*, the drink of fermented yucca roots, and get drunk. We went far on a trail and killed people to take heads.

That's the way we used to do. Before you people came, that's the way we did. Then I heard about Jesus. They told me about God the Father. They told us His Word. "How can I keep on killing if I believe these things", I thought? Even though I used to be like that before I came to know God, after I received Jesus, I left those things behind. Jesus overcame me. My heart went "zing!" with joy.

People say to me, "Why don't you talk about killing anymore? Why have you, a powerful chief stopped killing? Why do you just talk about Jesus?"

"Now listen to me with your ears", I said. "You should do the same," I told them. "Live well. Let's love only Jesus. Let's have his understanding. Why should we live bad, and get drunk, and kill and hate? For our sins Jesus suffered and died to pay our debt to God. Why shouldn't we trust God? God lives on high. God made the beautiful stars and moon to see by night. That's why I love to talk to God."

Send people everywhere to teach them about Jesus. Send lots of people to all the places where Jesus isn't known. Teach everyone – especially those who don't know and love Jesus, those who live in ignorance.

Chapter 19 - The Anaconda Story

By Lorrie Anderson

I want to tell you about an encounter I had with an anaconda, a large non-poisonous snake, but first I want to tell you a little about them so you will understand the significance of that encounter.

The anaconda, along with the python, is a type of boa constrictor, and both belong to the same family of reptiles—Boids, to be exact.

The anaconda inhabits lakes, swamps, and rivers of tropical South America. They live to be 40 or 50 years old in the wild and they weigh up to 440 pounds. Vogel, who wrote in the Grzimek Animal Encyclopedia, told of a giant anaconda they saw in the Orinoco River, Venezuela, which was about 26 feet long and 3 feet in girth (that is bigger than around my waist.)

"The entire body of the anaconda, from the head to the tip of the tail, is a single muscle package, which enables the snake to gain a powerful hold on its prey. After seizing the prey and holding it with its long, sharp teeth, the snake wraps its coils around its prey and kills it by strangling, suffocation, or drowning, or by squeezing until vital blood vessels burst," Vogel says.

"The large anacondas usually attack very small prey that they can easily overcome and swallow. They go after larger animals only when they are quite hungry. The snake will attempt to hold firmly to the animal and strangle it, but will not release it. A snake can unlock its jaws, enabling it to open its mouth very wide to swallow prey much, much larger than itself. There are cases of anacondas attacking and devouring adult human beings in the Orinoco Delta, where incidents involving Indians have been authenticated," he adds.

Time will not permit my telling the details of numerous attacks on humans, some fatal, in our area. The Indians and I have had more encounters with anacondas than I care to remember, but there is time for details of only one—my most memorable.

My partner, Lila, and I had been up at 5:30 a.m., so I could get breakfast while she taught Chief Tariri reading. By the time I got around to my devotions it was 9:30. Since Chief Tariri and his half-brother, Shiniki, were up on the roof mending thatch, I couldn't have my devotions in my bedroom. I went across the clearing to the Chief's to ask his wife where there was a quiet place I could read (a woman cannot go off by herself in that culture, or they think she's meeting her lover, so I had to ask Irina's advice, so she'd know where I was.) She said, "Why don't you go down to the lakeshore and sit in a canoe?" As I went, Shiniki suggested I sit in his canoe since it was a big, sturdy one, tied securely to the shore, and was not likely to tip over.

I went down to the steep bank and got into his canoe. (I was hidden from their view by the trees, but in full view of the people across the lake.) I looked around at the lake—the sun shining on the rippling water and the palm trees—and it was quiet and peaceful, and so beautiful! I said, "I must do this more often."

I had a lovely time singing a hymn, reading my Bible and doing a Bible study. I don't recall the passage, but it was about Elijah and his trials. I wrote in my notebook, "Sometimes we have to have time of trouble so we can see who God really is and what He can do."

Then I prayed, and had just started to pray for Old Chief Shutka when I felt this heavy weight thrown against me. By the time I opened my eyes to see what it was, the anaconda which was attacking me had already withdrawn for another strike. They had to get a good grip on their prey before they can wrap around them and squeeze them to death. His head was just even with mine—and I'll never forget those beady yellow eyes fastened on me, that enormous mouth opened wide, and those rows of tiny teeth with two long fang-like teeth, one on each side! He continued striking again and again, trying to get a good grip because I was struggling to get free. I was screeching at the top of my lungs *Isariya!* (anaconda!) but no one could understand me. They said they knew, however, what was attacking me, and they were sure it was the end. Just as he got a good grip on my left arm, he arched his back to wrap his coils around me. But just as he was ready to do so, he relaxed his grip and let go, slipping back into the water.

Now why do you suppose he did that? Various answers have been given, such as one in a popular magazine which said I fought it off. They didn't check with me, or I would have told them a woman doesn't fight off a snake which weighs two hundred pounds, and which has muscles strong enough to kill large jungle animals like alligators and jaguars. (A six-foot alligator was found inside an anaconda near our jungle base.) Some say my screams frightened him off, but wild boars scream louder than I, and besides have razor-sharp teeth, and yet anacondas kill and swallow them. These are all fierce fighters and can defend themselves well against most foes, so don't kid yourself that I fought it off! The Indians could hear me screaming two enormous fields away, and when my screams stopped, they were sure it was all over and that they would never see Monchanki again.

That large anaconda, which turned out to be over 16 feet in length and about 22 inches in girth, could have easily overcome me and squeezed me to death and swallowed me—but it let me go! The reason was that God said "Stop!" God had allowed the anaconda to attack me for His own purpose, but He would not allow it to kill me. There was still work for me to do. The Candoshi-Shapra New Testament was not yet completed, and the Indians were waiting to have God's Word in their own language. You cannot convince me that it was anything but a miracle of God—a miracle defying all the laws of nature. After all, that's what a true miracle is.

That's not the end of the story. After the anaconda let me go, I stepped out of the canoe onto the shore and stood there in shock. Lila was the first one there and led me back to the house. I was all covered with blood. It looked much worse than it was, since the wounds were superficial. She began bathing my wounds and just then some visitors arrived. It was Makawachi, an old witch doctor of the Quechua tribe, who had never been there before (nor did he ever come again), along with his daughter-in-law. They demanded to see Monchanki. The woman, pushing her way into the bedroom, took one look at me and they returned home. We didn't know what that was all about, and we didn't find out until sometime later, when they finally told Chief Tariri.

It seems that the old witch doctor was angry with us. That morning he had chanted to the spirit of the anaconda and sent it to kill me. I never used to tell this part, since not even Christians back then were aware of the power that Satan has that witch doctors and other evil men can call on. I firmly believed that Makawachi was able to do that—that the anaconda went to his bidding, and that, except for the power of God, it would have worked. Nothing else explains their visit. They would have had to leave their house about 3 hours before this incident happened in order to get there just after it happened.

Well, if you have your doubts forget this part and, in conclusion, let's come back to the purely physical power of an ordinary anaconda in the wild as described in the more dependable encyclopedias.

We see that the anaconda is a very powerful, sometimes aggressive giant snake, which is a formidable foe to any human being who happens to be there when it is hungry. Anyway, a large adult snake is able to overpower and kill a person and swallow him whole.

I can't believe that any hungry anaconda is going to drop his prey once it has overpowered it, but if this has never happened to anyone besides me, I am sure it was by the same power that delivered me.

After the anaconda's aborted attack on me, Chief Tariri of the Shapra-Candoshi tribe said, "The anaconda is very great and very powerful, but God is greater."

Chapter 20 - Shiniki:
The First Shapra Teacher

Chief Tariri was proud that some of his relatives were interested in education. His half-brother, Shiniki, became the earliest teacher of the Candoshi. He willingly trained at Yarinacocha three months each year so that he could teach in both Spanish and Candoshi. Some of his students, such as Yámpisa Shutka, later became teachers.

Two of the startled eyes watching Dorrie and me approach Tariri's village by canoe for the first time were those of Tariri's naked preteen half-brother, Shiniki, with bamboo sticks in his earlobes, a string of seeds around his neck, and a green parrot on his shoulder. We had never seen such a sight before.

No less astonished was his best friend, Tariri's crippled son, Tsirimpo. As Dorrie and I struggled to learn the Candoshi-Shapra language, both boys delightedly joined in the sport of teaching words and correcting pronunciation. We, in turn, taught Shiniki to read and write. When Peru's bilingual school system was started, each translation team was asked to send as many young people as possible to learn to be bilingual teachers. The only one who could read well enough to do this at first was Shiniki. Even then, he had to be tutored in his own language so that he could follow the courses in the program. He had never had the opportunity to learn Spanish.

Shiniki became a good teacher. He taught the children to read and write in their own Candoshi-Shapra language, and he also taught them arithmetic and social studies. Then he began instructing them in conversational Spanish. He willingly returned to Yarinacocha for three months each year for more training in order to stay ahead of his students.

There were no others to train for bilingual teaching until some had been taught by Shiniki. Yámpisa Shutka was one of the first of these. He was a youngster who, with his family, had escaped from enemies and settled near a lake. At age ten he started school, proved exceptionally bright, and eventually became a teacher among the upriver people.

* * *

Shiniki taught the Shapra for many years. He married a beautiful woman, Matika, when he was only eighteen years old. Matika was about ten years his senior, but the union seemed to work well. Together they raised a number of children including one retarded child who was not shunned by his family, but welcomed and nurtured.

Something happened to Shiniki when he was in his late twenties. He went into the woods alone, and returned battered and bruised, saying he had been beaten by an evil spirit. The marks on Shiniki's body could not have been done by himself. There was no clear explanation. Shiniki was very disturbed by the beating, and for a while was somewhat out of his mind. The next time he went to Yarinacocha for training, I took him on to Lima, the capital, to see a doctor. This didn't seem to help much, but Shiniki eventually settled down. From that time on, however, he suffered bouts of anxiety.

Shiniki was never quite the same after the incident in the woods. However, he lived out his life as a husband, father, and respected village teacher. His battle with evil did not keep him from the work to which he had dedicated his life. He was an important person in the education of the Shapra, bringing into the light both children and adults locked in the darkness of illiteracy.

By 1994, because of willing and capable Candoshi like Shiniki, the number of schools in that area reached twelve. Those first schools provided the early training for most of the future teachers.

Parts of this story were first published in "The First Candoshi Teachers," by Lorrie Anderson and Thelma Johnston, *Bridge Builders*, Cameron Townsend and others, SIL, 1994.

Old Shiniki

The following is an account that Old Shiniki told me shortly before he died:

When the girls came to live among us, we were pretty mean to them. They would ask us about our language, they would show us something, and ask, "What do you call this?" and we would tell them something different. We laughed at them a lot and really didn't help them. When they left in the plane, we all laughed and said, "They won't come back." But they did come back. Still, we didn't help them.

When they left the second time we laughed again and were quite sure they wouldn't come back, but they came back again. That third time they came we were all sick and some of us were about to die. They brought medicines with them and got us all well again, even the very sick ones. So, then we knew that they really wanted to help us and we began to listen to them. I feel ashamed of the way we treated them at the beginning.

Chapter 21 – Chief Tariri Visits Lima and the President

Adiós, Curaca **Tariri**

by Lorrie Anderson

Tariri, chief of the Shapras, had been chagrined all his life that he was not tall and stately. One of his rivals, Chief Shutka of the upper Pushaga River, was just that and Tariri envied him. Although Tariri was not tall, he was every inch a chief—his regal bearing, his demeanor all lent credence to the fact that he held a high position as war chief over seven rivers of the Shapra domain. Would you expect dignity from a mighty headhunter who not only speared his enemies to death, but took off their heads and shrank them for trophies? He *was* dignified, however, and was a leader of men, well-respected by them.

A Candoshi, of whom the Shapras were a sub-group, gained the title of *curaca* (chief) by killing an enemy; the more enemies he killed, the greater he was. But to gain and keep a following, he had to work harder than any of the others. He had also to talk louder and longer than the rest in order to have their respect. On all counts Chief Tariri passed muster.

In 1956, a Peruvian official, friend of Cameron Townsend, suggested a big celebration to commemorate SIL's original contract with the government of Peru. Chief Tariri happened to be at the center at Yarinacocha for a medical checkup for his little boy. He was invited to go to Lima, the capital, and participate in the anniversary celebration. Tariri accepted; he said that above all else he wanted to meet the big Chief of his nation.

Tariri met first with the president's representative and told him what he was like before—killing enemies, chanting to the anaconda, and living in fear until he gave his heart to Jesus. Arrangements were then made for him to meet the President.

The momentous day arrived, Chief Tariri, dressed in his one outfit of Western clothes, wearing a crisscross chest ornament of seeds, his ponytail adorned with rosettes of red and yellow toucan tail feathers and with earrings of iridescent green beetle wings dangling from his ears, was ready to meet President Manuel Odría.

Was Tariri nervous? No. He was very poised, completely unabashed by the awesome presence of the President, General Manuel Odría. He respected him, he was in awe of him to a certain degree, but he did not feel the least bit inferior. Weren't they both chiefs? Obviously, he felt every bit the President's equal. Chief Tariri said confidently and loudly, as is the Candoshi custom, "*Tamarimta, tarish? No taritamina.*" ("How goes it, are you alive? I am too.") The President answered with an *abrazo* and said, "Fine, and you?"

"What a shame," said President Odría, "that you don't speak Spanish."

"That's your fault," Tariri said coolly. "If you had sent us teachers a long time ago, we'd be able to speak Spanish. No one ever taught us until my sister Monchanki here (Lorrie Anderson) came."

President Odría was momentarily taken aback. Though Chief Tariri's answer was frosty, it was evident his attitude was not hostile, and the conversation continued on a friendly note.

Later at the final meeting, while the President's staff waited outside, Chief Tariri, along with Cameron Townsend and Lorrie Anderson to interpret, had a half hour with the President. The chief told the President the story of his conversion to Christ. He gave a vivid description of the changes in his life and in his tribe as a result of the Word of God coming to them.

Tariri mentioned how he no longer drinks tobacco juice and *chonta* (a type of chicha, a fermented drink from the fruit of the chontaduro tree). "I have told my people to destroy all of the tobacco plants in their gardens and not to make *kapóssi* (fermented manioc drink) anymore. I asked them to stop fighting and killing as God requires of us. 'Let's live in peace with each other,' I said."

Chief Tariri offered to clear land and prepare it for an airstrip and expressed a desire to further peace among the various faction in his tribe and between the various tribes of his area. He felt a rapport with General Odría and said of him, "I could see that the Chief's eyes were good." (He could tell from his eyes that he was trustworthy and dependable.)

The President gave him a farewell present of 150 machetes for the men of his and nearby communities, as well as thread for the women.

Cameron Townsend tactfully thanked President Odría for all that the government had done for the Indians and expressed appreciation especially for the bilingual school system in the jungle which was bringing literacy to Indians of many language groups there. Linguists of SIL were training Indian teachers who in turn were teaching reading, writing, and other subjects, to their fellow tribesmen, first in their own language and then in Spanish.

Later, speaking to educators, Chief Tariri proudly reported that his brother and his son were learning to read and hoped to become teachers. His half-brother, Shiniki Kasímoró Yatarisa, became the first bilingual teacher among the Candoshis. Tariri's son, Tsirimpo, became a medic and was much loved and appreciated until his death a few years later.

Every message Chief Tariri gave, every conversation he had, had to be translated by Lorrie Anderson into English then by Cameron Townsend in his beautiful grammatical Spanish. Ethel Wallis in her book *Tariri: My Story*, (p. 98) says "Surrounded by government officials, and by reporters eager to photograph the jungle chief so exotically arrayed in a combination of tribal garb and warm Western clothing to ward off the Lima cold, Tariri met every situation with poise and dignity. In one historic moment, while separated from his interpreters, he felt a strong urge to deliver a message. He did so for fifteen minutes, holding the crowd spellbound by an eloquent speech which no one present could understand. One account reported 'his pronunciation was energetic, accompanied by rare gesticulation and mimicry.'"

Almost daily something of Chief Tariri and his testimony appeared in the Lima newspapers. He also spoke by radio of his new life and his gratitude to the Peruvian government for letting believers bring the message of Christ to him and his people—all of the Shapras and Candoshis.

Cameron Townsend said, "I will never forget the witness Tariri gave to the President of the Republic, to the cabinet officers and to the newspapers. Don Pedro Beltrán, an outstanding Peruvian, owns a big newspaper. He received the chief in his office with his editorial staff around him. He began to talk with Tariri just as a tourist would to a strange-looking savage, until finally he said, 'Tariri, you have come in for your first trip to Lima. Perhaps you have a message for the people of this city.' Tariri replied, 'I do. I was a powerful chief but unhappy— always fighting and killing. These girls came, learned my language, gave me the Word of God. I let Jesus Christ come into my heart. I have been transformed. I love everyone now. I love the Indians, I love the other tribes, I love you white folks.' You should have seen Don Pedro— the look on his face! He turned to the other men and said, 'This must go in the paper. Take him into the editorial room.' Thus, the witness was published."

"*Adiós, Curaca Tariri*", with these words, *El Comercio*, one of the leading newspapers of Lima was saying goodbye to Chief Tariri. Lima will not soon forget your noble bearing and your message of love from the heart of and ex-savage.

Chapter 22 - New Life for the Candoshi

The Candoshi Indians of northeastern Peru are by tradition animists who live in constant fear of spirits. However, they do seek the power that spirits can give them. A young Candoshi seeks after spirit power so that he may become stronger than his enemies. The spirit of the jaguar, he believes, makes him a great killer and unafraid to go into battle. Some seek the power to be a good orator and have influence over other people. The spirit of the anaconda—the dreaded giant boa constrictor—to whom he may chant when a loved one of his or a neighbor's has malaria, gives him power to heal this disease. A man adorned with "trophy belts", made with the hair of enemies whose heads he has taken, has a reputation of possessing strong spirits. The spirits of the anaconda, jaguar, and the hawk, as well as the spirits of certain other animals, birds, and plants, give a man _arotama_ (the power of long life). This power protected him for the rest of his life.

But life among the Candoshis has dramatically changed since two single girl translators, Doris Cox and Lorrie Anderson, came to live in Chief Tariri's village. The chief himself has turned from appeasing the spirits to become a strong believer in Christ. He has quit raiding and killing and now exerts a powerful Christian witness.

Chief Tariri and other Candoshis have received new life in Christ. The word "life" in Candoshi (for example, in 1 John 5:12: _"He that has the Son has life. He that does not have the Son of God does not have life."_) denotes a lasting _quality_. To say, "one has life"," or "life is in him," in Candoshi doesn't merely contrast a man with a corpse. It means he has a quality of life which is enduring. This, the Bible translators say, is in contrast to the life and power which the "old ones" were seeking in chanting to boas, killing, shrinking heads, and in other rituals.

The Scriptures say in John 10:10b: _"I am come that they might have life, and that they may have it more abundantly."_

Chapter 23 - Tsirimpo, Son of the Chief

Tariri, Indian Chief of the Shapra Indian Tribe, way back in the jungles of Peru, was overjoyed. Perhaps someday his son, whom they named Tsirimpo, would be able to continue in his place as Chief of the Shapra tribe.

"How lucky I am", thought Marashu as she looked at her newborn baby. "He is my first baby, and he's a boy. How happy his father, Tariri, will be."

Tsirimpo lived with his mother and father in a jungle house with a dirt floor and grass roof.

Because Tsirimpo's language had never been written down on paper there were no books and no schools. Tsirimpo's schooling was learning to fish with a spear and hunt with a blow gun. He learned to hunt for a special palm tree in which he could find lovely white grubs to eat, and the heart of the tree was a special delicacy.

Tsirimpo learned very early in life the meaning of fear. When might some dreadful disease take them, or some fearful accident happen to them? They believed evil spirits entered into people and caused disease and even accidents, and knew nothing about medicine to cure diseases. True, they had some wild herbs that they used as medicines which sometimes helped.

Tsirimpo's father had another wife besides Tsirimpo's mother, and so, there were other children in this family that were only half-brothers and half-sisters to Tsirimpo. But when he was about 8 years old his mother had another baby boy, Oroshpa.

Every now and then the whole tribe had a big party. Days beforehand, Tsirimpo's mother, Marashu, would cook up a big clay pot of yucca, a vegetable somewhat like the potato. Then she would chew some of it and spit it into the pot and at the same time mash it with a chomper made of wood. The chewed-up yucca would turn sour, ferment into something called *masato*, and then it would be just right for the big party. Dancing to the beat of drums and drinking would last all night. Along with the *masato* they sometimes drank juices made from other jungle herbs. Tsirimpo was especially happy this night. He had been allowed to drink some of the jungle herb juice at the big party for the first time in his young life. He began to feel he was growing up.

And then a strange thing began to happen to Tsirimpo. At first it was barely noticeable, but it seemed the muscles in his lower legs were beginning to pull and shorten. This was the first dreadful thing that had ever happened to Tsirimpo. As time passed his heels pulled up so that he couldn't walk on them and slowly he began to shift his balance to the balls of his feet. Now he was strange looking indeed. Tariri said, "If we had known you were going to be a cripple, we would have killed you when you were born. But how could we have known."

Tsirimpo knew his father was beginning to be ashamed of him as he became crippled. This was the second dreadful thing that happened to Tsirimpo. But he knew his mother would never stop loving him. But before long, the third dreadful thing happened to Tsirimpo. His mother, the only one who really loved him, died. It is a custom in this tribe that the father must pay more attention to the children of his living wife than the children of his dead wife, so Tariri provided food for Tsirimpo and Oroshpa but paid no more attention than that to them. Tsirimpo had to take complete care of Oroshpa, even in his crippled condition. His heart began to grow more and more bitter, and he questioned. "Why did these things happen to me?" His bitterness was so strong it even began to twist his face into ugliness.

About this time two foreign girls with white skins came to ask if they could live in the tribe. Chief Tariri said, "What can two helpless girls do to harm us? We will let them live here." Tsirimpo tells us about these girls. They listened to our words, and then wrote these words on little slips of paper and tried to say them. They had a very hard time at first saying anything right. But they never gave up. Day after day they studied. After a while we noticed they always read a lot from a certain book they had with them. When they learned enough of our words, they told us it was a book that had in it God's Words, and they wanted to put these words into our language so we could understand them.

We wanted to know very much what God's Word said, and they tried very hard to put bits of it into our words. Some of it sounded good but some of it we didn't like because it pointed out the wicked things we thought and did. But then they told us about Jesus, God's Son, who came to earth and lived here a while, and then died and came back to life again, and then went back to heaven to be with God. They said He died for us so that we might be forgiven for all those wicked things we did and said. If we would just believe Him and receive Him into our hearts and lives, they said He could change our hearts so we wouldn't want to do those things anymore. Then when we died, He will take us to heaven to live with Him forever.

Tsirimpo was thrilled with the story the girls told about Jesus being God's Son and how much Jesus loved them, even Tsirimpo himself. But could he believe all of these? Surely his mother was the only one that could love someone as ugly as he, and now she was dead. But the girls kept insisting that Jesus did love him. Tsirimpo kept saying to the girls, "I wonder who will be the first to believe and receive Jesus." "Maybe it will be me". When the girls explained that he could decide to believe and receive Jesus right then, both Tsirimpo and Tariri's wife, Irina, seemed to think it was just too simple. Or maybe it was that Tsirimpo wanted his father to receive Jesus first. And then one day Tariri did receive Jesus and he went right to his wife, Irina, and the other children and told them all about it. Tsirimpo wasted no time but hurried right to the girls and said he wanted to believe and to receive Jesus, too.

There was a great change that came into Tsirimpo's personality from that time on. He became happy again and lost his bitterness and his face once again wore a happy smile. He knew now that Jesus loved him and had come to live in his heart forever. This was the first really wonderful thing that had happened to Tsirimpo. But there was one ache in his heart that would always be there. If only his own dear mother had lived to hear the Gospel too. Where was she now?

After Tariri received Jesus, he was changed too. He no longer wanted to kill his enemies, and get drunk, and do other wicked things. He slowly began to be kinder to Tsirimpo, and as he came to know Jesus better, he also began to love and appreciate Tsirimpo more. This was the second wonderful thing that happened to Tsirimpo.

And then, several years ago, a third wonderful thing happened to Tsirimpo. The girls told him they were praying about sending him to their country where he could get an examination to see what had caused him to be crippled, and maybe there they could even fix his feet. Tsirimpo hardly dared to hope. Finally, the day came to leave. Tsirimpo was frightened leaving home and family and going to a strange country. He knew people all over would stare at his feet, and he couldn't wear shoes. What if it were cold in this other country? But he felt anything was worth getting his feet straight like other people's.

On to the Mayo Clinic he went. After exhaustive tests the doctors decided it must have been some narcotic herb juice that Tsirimpo drank too much of at some time that caused him to be crippled as he was. Then he remembered the big party. They said they would try to straighten his feet by cutting them in a certain place. How could they possibly ever do that? They gave Tsirimpo something to make him sleep and after one operation on each foot he was able to walk with his feet flat on the ground like normal people. What a thrill it was! Workers at Wycliffe that knew about Tsirimpo and were personal friends of the girls supplied the money that was needed to pay for the trip and the operation.

Today he is studying in Bible School and wants to go to a new location where some of his own people live and teach them God's Word. All they have of God's Word is the New Testament.

Chapter 24
The Pull of the Old World on Yámpisa

Yámpisa: The Pull of the Old World on a New Christian

I had known Yámpisa since he had run away from Old Shutka's up-river tribe with his mother and siblings, when Yámpisa was a young boy. They settled in Chief Tariri's area. Yámpisa was a student in the first school in Tariri's village, and he became like a son to me. As he matured, he studied to become a teacher, and often came with me to Yarinacocha to help me with translation. The following story illustrates how difficult it was for new Christians to break away completely from the old ways of Shapra culture—to leave behind the darkness and superstition of the violent pagan way of life they were born to.

Yarinacocha, Tuesday, April 7, 1964

This afternoon, talking with Yámpisa, he was telling me how he learned to chant to the boa and a few other things he had learned at Siquanga. He wanted to *kamota* (ingest drugs) for *zotamaama* (casting spells) to heal children. He came very close to *kamoting* (ingesting drugs), but God kept him from it. He wanted very much to be a witch doctor so he could bewitch Sikonta and kill her. He said: "I am very bad. I did so many bad things. That's why I want to kill myself". I asked him what he wanted to escape? He said, "sins of the past". I told him not to think of suicide, not to consider it at all, because if he does, the day might come when he is sick and discouraged as *mankish tsipat ashik* (in his heart he felt like dying) and he could kill himself.

He says he does think of it often, almost every day. He says he was so bad, and he is ashamed. He said if God scolds me in heaven, I'll just stand behind a tree and listen, ashamed. But when he gets a chance, he will speak up. That is if his heart is like it is now (meaning, I think, if he is conscious as he is now). He tells God, "It's true I was very bad, but I love You and You can do with me what You want. You can punish me, cast me out or whatever you wish." I kept reminding him that the Lord will scold us about what we did wrong and will give rewards and crowns like *totayshiishi* (head-dresses) to those who work for Him. But

95

he will never cast his child out. He said that if there were a way to escape by killing himself, he would. But he knew there is no way to escape.

I asked, "Why do you want to escape?" "Because I am ashamed of my sins," he replied. I reminded him that he had just lived really badly like that for one year, and he could now live the rest of his life, maybe twenty years, for the Lord, and one would balance the other. That wasn't exactly what I said, but anyway, he got the idea of the number of years and that he could live the rest of his life for the Lord. He said, "sometimes I want to go back to the old ways (not his exact words, but the idea). But then I remembered the people and that they have no other way of to learn of God except through me." I asked him why he wanted to kill Sikonta. "Did you want to kill her even though you loved her?" He answered, "I wanted to kill her because I loved her. I did not want anyone else to have her. I said I wanted to get married. I'll live alone and *kamota*. I don't want her to marry anyone else. Even after a long time, if she gets married, I'll kill her by bewitching her." He asked, "Do you suppose it's possible to kill someone by Satan's power?" I said, "it may be possible." He said his heart was very bad. He said he told his mother what he wanted to do, and she said something like: 'How could you kill her?' And something else, I don't recall." He said he used to feel that way, but now he is *matiik* (contented). He said, "I can't forget her altogether. How could I? But I don't want to think bad about her anymore." He said that he felt ___? about his and Shovara's talking so much about the way they used to live, and the girls they did bad things with. He said, "I want to forget it [and I told Shovara this]. At first Shovara did not talk about it anymore, but now he's started, and he talks a lot about it now. That isn't good."

Yarinacocha, Friday, April 10, 1964

Yámpisa wavers between being joy to me and being the bane of my existence. Yesterday he was a terror. It was his *I hate women* day. Although I had not roused his ire, I was included in his wrath, being a woman. He felt very sorry he made me sad, and he straightened it all out with the Lord last night and with me this morning. I had suggested yesterday that maybe he was getting tired of staying here and working for me. So maybe he'd rather go out to Kilometer 15 (the teacher school) now. He was asking me this morning to tell him everything I thought in my heart when he was acting up yesterday.

I brought up the subject again, that perhaps he was tired of helping me and perhaps I bothered him with my nagging. He said yesterday he almost left. He said he thought of going home, getting his mosquito net and leaving for Kilometer 15 without saying anything. But he didn't for two reasons. One, it would a bad testimony to Chowika. He'd come and ask, "where is Yámpisa?" I would say, "I don't know, he didn't say anything to me." Chowika has just come here again, and he would not know what to think. Two, if I went away from here mad and in that frame of mind, I will not enjoy going to school there. It would spoil it."

He is maturing so much. The natural Candoshi attitude would be to throw a fit and take off. How I praise the Lord he did not. It would have upset all of us needlessly. He misunderstood my intention. I did not say it in anger, but he jumped to the conclusion that I wanted to send him away, tired of him, or as punishment. I was just giving him that alternative. Actually, I want to keep him here as long as possible, one, just because I like having him around, even if he is a brat at times. I appreciate the opportunity of teaching him. Two, I need his secretarial help. I wish so much I could record all of my conversations with Yámpisa, both good and bad. What a book it would make! But, of course, I would not dare to print every word of it for his sake, plus, he would not talk most of the time if he knew I would be recording it. But it is so rewarding, and so much of it is a blessing and joy.

Our conversations today were so good, like the one tonight when he told me about the blessings he received when we revised Old Testament stories, and as he read the Gospel of John for about an hour all by himself. He learned something about communing with God that many older American Christians have not learned. So, he's really an enigma.

He was telling me how he was going over the Ten Commandments. But it was the first one that especially spoke to him: Don't love anyone above me. And he said to God, "Who else would I love? There's no one else besides You." And then he said he laughed with delight. "I answered God just as if He were a person sitting there." (I think the spontaneity and naturalness of it delighted him.) He said he laughed with God a lot. He said that often, as he reads the Word, it tickles him and he laughs, not a laughter of disrespect, but of delight.

He had started out this conversation by saying, "As I sat all by myself reading from I John, I thought many things in my heart. I said to myself, God does exist. I can feel Him in my heart. I want others to see Him as I have seen Him. I know He exists by His Spirit who He has put within me. If I can reveal Him to others, then I will be happy."

Chapter 25 - Yámpisa

Handwritten Notes
The Prodigal Son Returns

Yámpisa Shutka hadn't planned to repent that day, making an about-face to recommit his life and follow the Lord again after years of bitterness and riotous living. It was the farthest thing from his mind. We had made the long, tiring trip to Unanchay the previous afternoon, in a large dugout canoe with a small motor, at the invitation of headman Tskimbo Bisa. Tskimbo was called away before we got there to help a sick friend downriver. Shiniki Kasímoró was his former bilingual teacher, and was in critical condition from an attack of "malignant" malaria (a particularly virulent strain of *falciparum* cerebral malaria.). Therefore, we didn't get to see my dear "son" Tskimbo, who is also far from the Lord.

Yámpisa came to see us at Tskimbo's house, where his wife, Payalli, was serving us *kapóssí*, their masticated yuca drinks, safe to drink because it was boiled. In reply to my inquiry about his health he joked about the good medicine he took daily—his fermented (unboiled) *kapóssí*. Yes, he would stay for church. He hung on every word of Arpi's as he gave a very good sermon from the Candoshi Scriptures. (They have no pastor and thus no church there.)

Because I was exhausted, and not feeling well, I just had to lie down after church under my mosquito net on the palm bark sleeping platform. "You aren't going to talk further with Yámpisa?" Gracie said. "No, I have to rest". But we had to leave there before dark that day.

Gracie began to talk to Yámpisa and his wife Yamachi about their spiritual needs. (Yámpisa is very fluent in Spanish. Yamachi understands nothing.) After a bit she opened her Bible to Isaiah 53 where it tells of the suffering Messiah would have to go through. As she read, Yámpisa's heart was broken as he contemplated the Crucifixion and the Lord's love for him, and he began to cry. This was a man who had gone his own way for 15 years, or more, resisting all attempts at reconciliation and hardening his heart all the more. Yámpisa had been like a son to me since he was a little boy, eventually helping me with translation. I prayed for him almost daily all those years, however many, that he went astray, snatching him back by faith from the hand of the enemy, Satan. Now my prayers were to be answered.

Gracie called to me. Yámpisa wanted to make things right with the Lord. So did Yamachi, though she was not the rebel her husband was. I got up and with Arpi we all walked to the open-air community house in the middle of a field where we could have privacy for Yámpisa to confess his sins, renounce Satan and pray to his Heavenly Father. Along the way, Arpi's sister, who lives at Noanchay, met me sobbing. She wanted to repent and ask God to cleanse her from her sins. Would I come pray with her? Gladly. I was relieved that I would not have to be in on a recital of all of the livid details of Yámpisa's sinful past. Arpi was with them to pray with him and counsel him. Gracie couldn't understand more than a few everyday words of Candoshi. I got back to them at the end of that just in time for Yámpisa's joyous prayer of recommitment. As we walked back to the house, he put his arm around Yamachi and said, "This is my wife, and we are going to be together forever. Please pray for Yámpisa—Satan will not stop trying to lead him astray—and for Yamachi and their 10 children, 2 of whom…

Chapter 26 - Medical Needs of the Tribe

When Everything Is Not Enough

For various reasons, we would sometimes fly to other villages in Candoshi territory. On one occasion we were brought to a village with a very sick baby. We tried what medicines we had, but the baby did not get well. The father wanted us to fly the baby to the clinic at Yarinacocha, but that was a difficult thing to arrange, both logistically and financially. The father was a very menacing presence. While I was working with the baby, he stood somber, looming over me, running his fingers up and down the blade of a knife he held in front of him. Dorrie was working someplace else in the village, and I felt a growing sense of uneasiness. It felt as if the father were saying: "You heal my baby, or else."

But in spite of everything I could do, the baby grew sicker and sicker. Finally, in desperation, I arranged to have the baby and the parents flown to the clinic at Yarinacocha. I accompanied them on the flight, working with the baby as we went. The parents were extremely anxious. Sadly, efforts at the clinic were unsuccessful, and the baby did not make it. I was surprised that the parents, who were nearly hysterical when the baby was struggling to live, were very calm once the baby died. It reminded me of King David who laid on the ground, fasted, and pleaded with God for his and Bathsheba's newborn son until the baby died. King David then rose, bathed, and ate, explaining that further mourning would not bring his son back to him. The Candoshi parents seemed to feel the same way. I was surprised and mystified that they did not take the little body home for burial, but buried their baby at Yarinacocha. They simply left the baby behind and moved on.

When the parents returned to their village, they resumed normal life, as if the whole episode had been a terrible dream. This commonsense attitude was puzzling given the parents' extraordinary attachment to their child. However, it was a relief to me that they did not blame me or the medical team at Yarinacocha for the child's death. Maybe they could see that we had done everything we could for their baby, and they accepted that sometimes everything is not enough.

Miracle for the Witchdoctor
Radio Script #98 B-14
By E.R.S

A Wycliffe Bible Translator nurse, Jeanne Grover, who works among the Aguaruna of Peru, became aware of a blocked channel in her relationship with the Lord. When she sought His face in prayer for her own spiritual condition, the Lord not only met the problem of her life, but His power began to flow in a wonderful way to meet life-and-death needs in the lives of the Aguarunas and Huambisas.

One of the Aguaruna Indian women had cancer. In the hospital in Lima, she received help. But many times, the woman wavered between life and death. Jeanne, who had accompanied her, prayed daily with her for her state of mind and health, and God worked in both Jeanne's heart and the woman's body, until both were aware of His blessing. In fact, He restored the Indian woman physically beyond the expectations of the many doctors involved in her case.

When Jeanne returned to the jungle, little Magwig, a former witchdoctor, met the girls at the airstrip. He looked thin and worried. He couldn't swallow, he told them. Magwig was sent in the plane to the Yarinacocha Clinic, where there were excellent missionary doctors. Following thorough examination, the Wycliffe doctors there at Yarinacocha agreed that Magwig had an inoperable tumor at the upper end of the esophagus. They could do nothing for him, and he prepared to return home to die.

Later, Jeanne again visited Magwig's village. Although she talked with his son, she refrained from asking about his father, fearing to start the awful wailing that accompanies the narration of a death. But that night at supper, the local schoolteacher entertained them with humorous reminiscences about the little old man, a strange way for an Aguaruna to talk about a person who had recently died, Jeanne thought. Finally, she could no longer contain her curiosity, so she asked, "Whatever happened to Magwig?"

Very seriously the schoolteacher answered, "Sister, the Lord healed him! He is all well and has gone to the mountains to tell his relatives." It seemed that on the very eve of Magwig's departure from the Yarinacocha Center, God had answered the prayers which many had made for him. Magwig's son had prepared food for his own evening meal when, to his great surprise, his father announced that he too was going to eat, although he had eaten nothing for more than two weeks.

"Pray with me," Magwig requested his son. When they had prayed together, the little old man picked up his spoon, *"and everything sent space*," was the way he described it. He ate a hearty meal that night and has enjoyed his food ever since.

"Praise the Lord," said Jeanne fervently. Her prayers had been answered.

Radio Script #98 B-14
Pp. 382-3
Author: E.R.S.

"Fairy Drummer"
by Lorrie Anderson

Doris Cox and I had been out with the Shapras only a year or two, and David and Nancy Beasley invited us over to where they were living and working with the Huambisas. The survey team that had gone out to contact the Shapras also contacted the Huambisas and the Chayahuitas at the same time. Harold Goodall and Dave Beasley went first to the Chayahuitas and arranged for Harold and Juanita to go there. Then they went up to the Huambisas and arranged for David and Nancy to work there, then down to the Shapras, arranging for Doris Cox and me to work there.

We had been out for ten months, I think. We got special permission to stay out longer than usual, which is 6 months. We ended up being away from the jungle base for eleven months straight, but with a break at the Beasleys'. We were there for Christmas Eve, and we were sitting around, eating popcorn, had our little flares lit, and all of a sudden, we heard the sound of a very little drum beating. We looked out the window, and at the top of the hill beyond their house we saw this beautiful Huambisa lady, very fairy-like in her appearance.

She had long black hair and little, puffball earrings; they were from the breast feathers of the wild turkey, and her face was painted with red (achiote/paprika). She was singing a little song as she came down the hill. When she got outside our house, she did a little pirouette; she danced around in this little dance and continued singing the song that was so charming and so magical that we were just entranced with her. Then she went on. I just fell in love with Suwa, and her husband, Yampiki, who was a nice-looking Huambisa man who had kind of a deer-like face, wide-set eyes, a kind of aquiline nose, and who wore his hair long like they do. I got better acquainted with them and hoped they would be the first Huambisa believers, but they were not; there were others who came to the Lord first.

The next time we saw Yampiki, I believe Melba Greene was out with me. Doris Cox was maybe in a workshop, but anyway, Melba and I went out on the Morona River, I'm not sure why, maybe we went downriver with the Indians who were going to fish, or something. Along came a group of Huambisas, and among them was Yampiki, who had evidently gotten tuberculosis, but we didn't know what it was. He had these holes in his chest and neck; I forget what they call them, they don't call them holes. But anyway, we didn't know what it was, but it was just terrible. I was very distressed. They said they were taking Yampiki for treatment some place, to some witch doctors. We said, "Oh, he's not going to get better if he can't be taken to the jungle base; let us ask our doctor and ask Dave Beasley's permission to take him in to the base." So, we called, and got permission from Dave and Nancy, and the administration, the finance office, and the clinic, to bring him in there.

We took him in, and Dave and Nancy took care of him. It was tuberculosis, as I said; it was diagnosed as that; he was given the medicine (back then, the TB medicine worked very well against it.) David was able to use him as his language helper, and that was the beginning of a long relationship between Dave and Nancy and that couple. Yampiki got completely better, it appeared, and was better for many years, and helped Dave with the language and I believe, the translation too. One day Suwa and Yampiki became believers. Eventually, after many years, Yampiki did die; I believe the tuberculosis came back. But we loved them dearly and were happy that they came to the Lord and were able to be of help to David and Nancy.

Chapter 27 - A Baby Is Born!

Typed Journal Entry
Monday-Tuesday, July 20-21, 1959

[The account of one day and one night among the Piros. The first birth I ever "assisted" at.]

1959
Journal Monday, July 20, and Tuesday, July 21

Started off the [day] by writing letters as soon as I got out of my [mosquito] net, and before making my bed or eating breakfast. Gishonki was to leave early, and I wanted to get a letter written to Memogi and to my family so he could take them downriver with him. To write a letter to my boy Memogi is no small matter. I not only have to sit down, and remember all the numerous things I have been wanting to tell him for the past few weeks or so since the last letter, but I have to think what to say about it and just how to say it in Piro. So, it is not the least bit like sitting down and dashing off a quick, newsy letter to my family. It takes a lot of thought, but I'm quite thrilled that I am able to sit down and write a letter of such length in Piro.

Each time I have written to him I have written a four-page letter—hand lettered on folded writing paper. I have written each one almost entirely by myself and can say just about anything I want to say. I asked either Esther, or one of the Indians, if I wanted to say something in a better, or smoother way, grammatically. I wonder how my letters sound to Memogi when he receives them. He probably gets some good laughs, but I still would rather write them just by myself even if they aren't always perfect. It's such fun to write letters in Piro.

We took time out from our letter writing to eat breakfast. I didn't want to because Gish[onki] had said he wanted to leave at 8 o'clock. (By the way, he and Esther finished the second draft of the Gospel of Mark in Piro yesterday. Therefore, he is free to go back down river to his family and new baby boy. That is why he was so anxious to get a good start today.) However, it is good that we ate because it was late before he was able to leave. Esther had to correct his songbook and add the new songs which he has written. Then she had to straighten out accounts with him.

This all took most of the morning, and I was glad because it gave me time to write a long letter to Memogi, and quite a long one to the family. I wonder if they will ever get that letter. It is so uncertain writing and sending letters downstream by canoe to Atalaya and then from there by a plane which may come once a week or once in 6 months. However, from now on Doris and I are going to try to have letters ready all the time—brief, unimportant ones (so that it won't matter if they get lost) and whenever an Indian or Peruvian comes through going downstream, we can send one. That way our parents will at least get mail somewhat regularly even if it is old and late. The last we were able to send mail out by plane, which is the only safe and dependable way, was on April 26. That's a long time and it looks like the next time it will come, according to the radio, is on September 14.

Finally, Gishonki (my recording pupil) left and Huacha (I did not know his real name then) came to translate with Esther. Doris made dinner and I went off to teach. Gishonki was the first Piro believer, led to the Lord by Dr. Altig at our Yarinacocha clinic. Esther did the first basic translation in the Piro language with him. Our days since Tuesday have been so busy, and I've been so tired at night that I haven't written my journal since then. I must have gone to teach Gancha, and read Scripture with her, because I recall Doris called me to dinner while I was there. After dinner we didn't have our prayer meeting there, because Esther wanted to get right to translating. Huacha stayed home from hunting and fishing with the men, just to work with her, and then this morning she was occupied most of the morning.

So, we decided we'd postpone our prayer until tonight. I went to teach some of my pupils again. I guess I went and taught Virginia first, and then over to Nato's to teach her. I had just about finished teaching her, and she'd said she was tired, so we were just visiting. She was over at Losimila's house, and we were sitting up on their high platform.

Doris came along and stood at the edge of the platform and said, with kind of a dead-pan expression, "Now don't get excited, or say anything, but the baby is going to be born tonight. I was over there with Mashta (whom we call the "wood sprite" because that's what she's like). Pipcho has been having the pains and has been crying. I asked Pipcho and she said, yes, it was true, and she was quite sure that it would be born tonight. Now don't say anything or tell anyone because she doesn't want anyone else to know. Only Mashta (who is her closest friend) knows, and we three, because we're going to help her."

I didn't bat an eyelash but just said calmly and matter of factly, "Okay. What time is it?" About 4?" "Yes." "I just finished teaching so I'll leave now, and we can be getting things ready." Losmila, who was also there (in fact, it's her house), said, *klunernu*? (meaning "what is it?" or "what did she say?") I said, "It's four o'clock." They said something about cooking, and I said "Yes, it's my turn to cook." because it was. Then Doris and I left together.

Then followed a time of feverish preparation. If we could have torn around as if we were expecting a baby, it wouldn't have been quite as difficult. But we were supposed to be calm and nonchalant as if nothing were amiss. We had to be appearing to be going about our duties just as we did every other afternoon and evening. We have just one log fire going all the time as well as the Coleman gasoline stove which we use as little as possible. But we had plenty of firewood for a change and so I made two big log fires and put water on both. On one of them I put a great big Indian pot full of water. Esther was still translating with John up on the platform and he suspected that something was up by our excited talk as hard as we tried to be calm. He also said, *klunernu*? but Esther just ignored the question and continued to work. Doris and I began to gather together all the numerous things we'd need, and when Esther finished working, she helped.

We got out the book (by that I mean the only one we had with anything at all on the subject—which is a nursing book). We had already decided to some extent what each of us was going to do but we kind of changed that around a little, and Doris sat down making out a little slip of paper on what each of our duties were and what equipment we'd need. Esther was to receive the baby. As soon as the head appeared she was to run her finger quickly and gently around the baby's neck to make sure the cord wasn't around and would choke it. And then she was to hold her hand on the place where it might tear. Then she was to catch the baby, and hold it while Doris tied the cord and cut it. Then I was to immediately take the baby off and put it into its bed, dress the cord, and take care of it while the others took care of the mother. One of them was going to receive the placenta—Doris I guess, and she was going to massage the mother until the hard lump appeared. Esther was going to clean up and after that we were each going to fill in where we were needed.

But for the main part and the exciting part, we wanted to be sure that each one of us knew what she was going to do and when. This book told us some of the things we wanted to know, but it was for nurses, of course, and so it didn't tell how to deliver a baby, which the doctor usually does. It did give some good lists of what you'd need for the doctor and nurse both. So, we based our equipment on those lists. Doris made out a list of what each person would need for her jobs, so we each got those things together and ready. She had gotten quite a number of them ready the week or so before, when they'd first asked us if we'd help.

In between all of this I was trying to make supper. Of all time they had brought us fresh fish, which always has to be used right away, or it doesn't keep. I had to take time to cut off the heads, clean them, and cook them. I had a hard time concentrating on supper since we were all rushing around and talking about what we had to do, and trying to get things ready and sterilized.

Finally, we got just about everything ready, and supper was ready. We sat down and ate. Esther was saying how nice it was that we had left our daily prayer meeting until the evening that day so we could have it after supper and pray especially about our "project" of the evening. But we didn't know then that we wouldn't get to have our prayer meeting for that day.

Right after supper we had to go for a walk in the woods (we have no outhouse and so we have to go for these little walks in the woods numerous times a day) and sometimes they turn out to be jaunts, in order to have any real privacy. I think this is one of the few inconveniences of the mission field which really bothers us. On our way back we passed Pipcho's house and so decided to drop in and see how she was coming. Doris and I carried over necessary equipment, bottles, and basins, the box and cloths for the baby, large cans full of sterilized things, pails, and our large Indian jug.

Most of the people behaved and didn't ask questions, but our dishwasher asked if Pipcho was having pains. We had promised Pipcho we wouldn't tell anyone that the baby was coming tonight, but I couldn't lie so I said, "Yes." and no more. Then while she was still doing dishes, Teresita came over, who is our girlfriend—one of the closest in the village, and we just hate to have any secrets from her. She noticed that we had two Indian log fires going and came over to be nosey and said, "Oh, two fires." And then, as she entered the kitchen, which is on the ground floor (and I do mean dirt floor), she said, "No, three fires," as she saw that the Coleman stove was also lit.

Then, while she was still there, I had to light the other burner, making four. She said, "Oh, are you cooking?" and since I was pressuring a second batch of fish which some "kind" person had brought, I said again, "Yes" and no more. Then quite a bit later, as I stumbled along in the darkness so as not to attract attention, Isolina—the chief's wife—startled me by suddenly appearing in the darkness and saying: "Where is Losimila, has she left?" She knew perfectly well that she must have left long ago, but it was a good way to introduce the subject. She said, "I went to your house to look for her and she wasn't there, and none of you were there, nobody at all." I was noncommittal, so she went on to say, "Is the baby coming tonight?" I said, "Maybe, we don't know," which of course, was true since it might not happen, since there are often false alarms. Before the night was over, we began to think it was a false alarm.

When all of the paraphernalia had been carried over, I put out the last light in our hut and left a large pail of water on one fire and a small pot on the other log fire, then went over to join the others huddled on the floor with Pipcho in her little room. It was a cold night. We had had a spell of cold weather—so cold that most days we could hardly keep warm no matter what we put on, and some nights had to wear 2 or 3 pairs of pajamas. Jungle nights are almost without exception cold, but this was colder than usual, and I wondered why the baby couldn't have picked a warmer night, or nice sunshiny day.

When we first went over there it was about seven, and now it was about nine. The pains were about ten minutes apart, and we expected that soon they would be closer and then we could expect the baby any minute. As I mentioned before, the room was small and almost filled by the large mosquito net. The church building is made up of two rooms and in one of these live Gotsa (which means "long string" in Piro) and Pipcho (which in Piro is the name of a big green worm) and family.

There is a passageway in between these two rooms and the doors are off that. The rooms are up on a platform. In this passageway usually sleep Mashta, her husband, and two children, as well as <u>Nxolopi</u>, a boy of 14, and often other visitors. I think it was the Lord's working that took Nxolopi away on a fishing trip of several days with the chief and also made it possible for Mashta's new house to be finished across the river so she could move in today. Most of the men of the village were away fishing, or working. The Lord was good and had worked all things out so it would be convenient.

Pipcho was sitting beside the net, and Esther was next to her so she could see part of her face, and I was next to Esther. I could see the shadow of Pipcho's profile, which the light cast upon the mosquito net.

Doris was next to me. I said to Esther: "How can you tell when she has a pain?" For as far as I could see, or hear, having only just arrived, there was no sound or visible sign. Esther said: "She just catches her breath, that's all." Then she indicated the next time, and we timed every one. During her whole time of pain, I heard no cry out of her—only twice I heard a whispered, *gaya!* (pronounced "guy ya!") which is their equivalent of *ouch!* or something like that. Then on one occasion when the pain was quite bad, she whispered to Esther, *kachindu* (it hurts).

And so, the night passed! From the evening until nearly 4:00 am the next morning, we kept our vigil. We hardly talked and then we whispered. We were horrified to find shortly after we went over there that her two other children, Migami, a boy about age 5, and Lache, a girl about age 3 or 4, were under the mosquito net. We heard one of them cough and I said to Esther, "My goodness, what are we going to do with the children?" She replied, "I already remarked to her about them, and she says they'll be alright. She doesn't intend to make any noise and says they'll sleep thru."

Most of the night Pipcho just sat there quietly and when the pains came there was just that catching of breath. As I watched the shadow of her profile, I could see her bite her lips, or hold her mouth firm. She was wonderful. And then all the way through little Lache kept whimpering, sometimes in her sleep, and sometimes not. Pipcho would lean over and lift up the net and pat her or even bring her out into her lap. We three finally stretched out on the hard palm floor, and slept fitfully. In the middle of the night, I got chilly and went and put on a sweater and brought back my old chenille robe for Pipcho, who had nothing on but an old mended raggedy dress. And it was a cold night. It was kind of eerie there too—the three of us, and Pipcho, sitting there so quietly and the tiny kerosene lamp casting long shadows on the palm board walls and floor of that tiny room.

I guess we sat up all the time until about 12:00. From then on, we slept fitfully, lying down on the bare, dirty floor. We didn't care, we were so tired. About that time Pipcho went inside the net and tried to rest some and to quiet Lache. The pains weren't getting any closer together and we began to wonder if it had been a false alarm and the baby wasn't coming at all that night.

But a little before ------oh, I forgot, I guess Esther thought it really was a false alarm, because she gave up and went home. She knew she'd have to work on the translation the next day and so didn't want to lose any more sleep than necessary. She told us to call her as soon as the pains got really close. Doris and I slept fitfully on the floor, and when the pains got quite close Doris woke me up, and kept saying, "Lorrie, don't go to sleep." That was around 3:00 am, and shortly after that, when we thought something would happen any moment, Doris went to call Esther. I thought they'd never get back. I thought I'd be left to deliver the baby all alone. But they finally came. And we sat there waiting.

A little before 4:00 am, Pipcho asked Esther if we had a little *pgamlu* that she could have. Esther couldn't quite understand because that is the word for perfume, or something that smells. For some strange reason or other it clicked with me that she meant tea. I guess maybe she also said something about hot when Esther couldn't understand the other word. There is no word for tea in their language since they don't have tea, but they do know about it. I did give some to Elmira (one of the women of the village) when she was sick once. I also had wondered if she didn't want a hot drink to warm her up. So, I offered to go get the tea. I shouldn't have stayed so long, but I did. The village was so quiet and peaceful as I walked through the darkness to our house. When I reached there, our fire had gone down so much that the water was not very hot. I wanted the tea to be nice, and besides we only had only one portion of tea left, so the water had to be boiling well so it would steep well. (I'm writing this portion of the diary in red just to show Teresita, who is sitting beside me and wanted to know where the ink came from.) I took time to get the water boiling and also to build up the other fire with the big pail of real hot water. (That is, we wanted it real hot, but it wasn't boiling yet). Suddenly, in the stillness of the night, I heard Doris' and Esther's voices—not real loud, but more or less excited. I wanted to rush right over and now I wish I had, but I didn't, I stayed and finished my job.

When the tea was ready, I went over and just as I reached the steps of their house, I heard a cry which made my heart skip two beats. It was, "Wa, wa wa!" It couldn't be the new baby—not yet. When I had left just about 5 or ten minutes before, the pains were no worse or closer than they had been for hours. I thought perhaps it might be Lache crying, but it sounded more like a new baby. Then I heard, mingled with those cries, Lache crying too. I clambered up the log steps and slipped quietly into the room. I couldn't see anything at first because the large heavy mosquito net was between them and me. I stood there for a moment, stunned. Things had happened so fast. I stood frozen, almost afraid to look, listening to the mingled sounds—the cry of a new baby,

Lache's frightened cries ("What are they doing to my mother?" she must have been thinking), Esther's and Doris' low but excited voices.

[July 21? (This must be July. (When you read this, you'll understand why I hardly knew the date.)]

Suddenly I aroused myself out of my lethargy saying to myself, "Get over there. What are you waiting for? You've waited weeks for this opportunity, don't waste a moment."

I went, but I haven't been able to remember since just what happened—it's all a blank. I guess the excitement dazed me. However, I was calm and did the things I was supposed to do—but I guess it was more like moving around in a dream. I just remember a few details vaguely. I came around the corner of the net, and in the little space of three feet by six, behind the net, was Pipcho kneeling with a look of horror on her face (I was surprised because up to now she had shown no fear but I learned later she had reason for that look)—Esther was stooping down with the baby in her hands and Doris was tying the cord (that enormous cord which was 5 times bigger than we expected.) I could barely see the baby. I must have gone over and gotten all the things ready that I needed. I was to take over the baby as soon as the cord was tied and cut. I must have taken the things out of the bed (cardboard box lined with lots of rags and flannel and blue cloth on the sides). I must have arranged the things and filled the hot water bottle, etc. But don't ask me, I don't remember.

Esther and Doris told me later what had happened while I was gone. Pipcho was inside the net, Esther and Doris were sitting outside. I hadn't been gone very long when they heard a swish—the water breaking. Esther wanted to run and get me so I wouldn't miss anything, and according to the books there should have been time. But Doris fortunately said, "No, wait, if anything happens, we'll both be needed."

Hardly 5 minutes later there was another SWISH! and a little thud on the floor. They rushed around the edge of the net and Esther, who reached there first, picked up the tiniest, newest Piro from the dirty, cold, splintery palm board floor and held her in her hands. Pipcho was kneeling just outside the net. (Piro women don't lie down to have their babies, they kneel. They usually go out in the woods and kneel and hold on to a tree. When the baby comes, they place a rock on the side of the cord near them, cut the cord with a sharp rock or a *wata* (a sharp grass), and tie the cord with vine or a string they brought along.

Sometimes they call for their mothers, or another close person for help, but they quite often have their babies alone. This is the way the Piro women always had their babies in the past and some still do, especially the more primitive ones upriver. Those who don't go out to the woods have their babies under their nets if there aren't people around. These people are very quiet and modest about births. The Chontal Indians (a Mayan tribe from Tabasco, Mexico) all crowd into a room and watch when a woman is going to have a baby, but these women want to be alone, and the others respect their desire for privacy. For this reason, we didn't get our desire to witness and assist with the actual birth. However, in Pipcho's case it happened so fast that there wouldn't have been much to see and surely nothing to do, so, actually, we only missed a few minutes.

Pipcho had already placed the rock on the cord toward her side, expecting us to tie just the side near the baby. But of course, we expected to do as we were taught by the books. Doris tied it in one place, but Pipcho thought it should be tied closer to the baby, so Doris let her tie one, thinking she might know how to tie a better knot, and besides, it might relieve her nervousness. Then Doris tied another one to be sure. Pipcho wanted it cut right close to the baby, but Doris ignored that request and cut it about 3 inches away as we had been told. Right in the middle of all this—the most important part and the part that required the most concentration—the mosquito net caught on fire! (We had brought over a closed-in kerosene lantern so that nothing like this would happen, but Pipcho had set her little lamp with the open flame out there and in the excitement of course, no one changed them around.)

At that moment, for the first time, Pipcho lost her calmness and got excited. She wasn't afraid for herself—but for her little boy and little girl as well as for her tiny, new baby. She batted at it with her hands and Doris moved the light and she and Esther crumpled it in their hands until it went out. That accounted for the look of horror that was on Pipcho's face when I entered.

It was after the fire, and then after I got there and got the bed ready, that the cord was finally cut, and Esther said, "She's ready, come and get her." I said, "is it a girl?" "Yes". I went and reached down to take her from Esther's arms, but she looked so frail and slippery, that I was sure I'd drop her and break her, so I said, "You put her in the box."

From then on, the baby was my responsibility. I had her all to myself. Esther and Doris were busy rushing around with other things— Doris massaging Pipcho while waiting for the placenta, and Esther cleaning up and trying to calm Lache. What did I do first? I guess I put a mild boric acid solution in her eyes, which I had made, since we didn't have the nitrate of silver solution. I tried to keep her covered as much as I could with the warm sterile flannel—it was so cold, Then I dressed the cord. I put Merthiolate on the end and then a dressing soaked in alcohol. Hated to put cold things on her tiny tummy. She was so cute—gooey as she was, black hair, lots of it—so shiny and black slanting eyes.

Agosto 11: I think I'll have to send this without finishing. She's now a big healthy girl. They named her Ntori, after Doris, her god mother, and in Piro *shi*: "monkey's pet."

Love, Doris
[P.S. I was still "Doris" to my family back then.]

Here comes the plane!

Chapter 28 - Young Rebel Finally Says "Yes" to God

Shooni was angry! His sister, anxious to get back at him for something, had called him a dirty name, one of the worst things you could call a Shapra boy or man. It wasn't true! He wasn't like young Uncle Wautista, who claimed he was given cocaine and molested by some men when he was away at boarding school at the town on the big river. Shooni wrestled his sister to the ground. Then he grabbed a *vasapa* (a fishing spear) and stabbed her. It was only a flesh wound. He was glad. At the moment he hated her, but he didn't really want to kill her.

The hostility and cruelty, however, were a pattern for fourteen-year-old Shooni. He told me how recently he had gotten into his canoe to go fishing, and his little brother came along, saying pleadingly, *Kayanotamta* (take me with you.) He couldn't be bothered. He was a pest. "No," he shouted, and as his brother attempted to get in the canoe, he gave him a shove and pushed off from shore. "My little brother screamed, 'ai!' and fell into the water," he says. He flailed his arms and swam toward the canoe, but Shooni paddled fast and left him behind crying his eyes out. "Why did you do that?" "Because I delighted in hating him" (literally "I deliciously hated.")

We might not have guessed what Shooni was like because when he came to our hut at Shoroya in the evening, to be recorded with the rest of the boys in Gracie's singing group, he was a charmer. And he had a lovely voice—the best of the boy sopranos. But when we spoke to him of surrendering to the Lord, it was no go. Though boys and girls and adults from every family were coming saying they wanted to make things right with God, Shooni resisted. He was from a family of rebels.

Shooni is a leader, so when he went to church only for the singing, and slipped out before the prayers and the sermon, most of the other boys did too. This was especially easy to do during evening services since the church is only dimly lit by a few kerosene flares. Sunday mornings they usually went hunting or fishing anyway.

But finally on one of the last nights we were there, Shooni came to our hut when most everyone had gone home. The Holy Spirit had pierced the armor of his hard young heart. Would everyone else please leave? They did. At least they left the house—they may have lingered in the shadows. But what did it matter?

Shooni's sins had been a secret to no one but us. However, his list was longer than anyone else's, except with the exception perhaps of Matika's, Simo's wife. There were no gross sins on her list, but many details—things that other people didn't think to admit to—wrong attitudes toward her husband, unfair treatment of her children, etc. Shoonie's list, like hers, showed insight and gave evidence of a genuine conviction by the Holy Spirit. The list included: hating his father, wrestling with him, fighting with his mother, beating up his brothers, getting drunk, dirty joking, smoking tobacco (but no drugs or other witchcraft, he said), and more, including the two incidents cited at the beginning. After that he renounced Satan and prayed.

I had not prompted him in the enumeration of his sins, nor did I coach him in his prayer. The words and thoughts were all his own. Here is an excerpt: "Father, break the chains with which Satan has bound me. Let your Holy Spirit come and fill me. We were not embarrassed to sing and dance for Satan. Don't let me be ashamed to worship you."

Please pray for Shooni along this line as there are those who will try to trip him up. Pray that he will stand firm and be a leader for the Lord God.

Shooni's mother was the first baby I saw when I went with Doris Cox to Chief Tariri's community on the Pushaga River, in 1950, but Nchiya had resisted the Lord all these years. Yaka, Shooni's, father a clown, had always been flippant about the Gospel, but this time he seemed different—more subdued. He said he wanted to talk and asked if we could come over to his house. We said we'd be there Sunday afternoon and started out, but before we got to deep ravine we'd have to go through to get there, a big storm came up and it poured. The children with us said we'd better try another day because we'd never make it up and down the slippery banks. When I apologized to Yaka the next time I saw him, he said it was O.K., he'd gone out in the woods and prayed by himself. I trust it was a true conversion. After that, Nchiya said she'd like to have her heart made right. These people like to have privacy when dealt with, so we planned to go over there. Before we could, we heard they were going on a trip and would not see them again. They'd already gotten into their canoe upriver, so when they came past the port downriver, we waved them down and said we'd like to pray with her. They got out of the canoe, came up the hill and we went into the thatch-roofed church, where she prayed to receive the Lord after confessing her sins briefly and renouncing Satan. Please pray for the rest of the family who are still holding out, especially 16-year-old Alejandro.

Chapter 29 - Angels Unawares

By Lorrie Anderson

Uncle Cam always urged us in Peru to be aware that we might be entertaining angels unawares (Hebrews 13:12). He cautioned us to never think that someone was unimportant, even the lowliest peasant. He and Elaine, when they lived in their temporary, makeshift housing on the edge of Lake Yarinacocha, invited in every Indian, (usually Shipibos), who passed by, for a cool drink. Later when their three-story home was finished at the Center there, the hospitality continued. Guests included Indians, local mestizos, Catholic priests and nuns, professors from the bilingual teachers training course, local officials, high officials of the national government, society people from Lima and so on.

Uncle Cam exhorted us to be friendly to everyone who appeared on the Center, to greet them, to direct them to where they needed to go, and to take time to make them feel welcome. No one is too insignificant for our attention. He may not look like anyone important, and may not be now, but you never know what he is going to become. He might be an official someday, he might even become the president of Peru! Who knows?

Uncle Cam was his own best example. One hot, dry day, a jeep arrived covered in dust, and an unassuming man jumped out. He didn't look like anybody in his nondescript clothes, but Uncle Cam treated him like royalty, never really guessing that he almost was. He turned out to be a general high in the Peruvian Army, and an influential one it turned out, when he went to bat for us against some enemies who were out to do us great harm, perhaps even throw us out of the country. But that's another story.

Recently we saw another example of Uncle Cam's principles at work in a report from Jim Wroughton.

Jim and Roy Peterson had an appointment with Peruvian Ambassador Ricardo Luna, at the Mission of Peru to the United Nations, in New York City. He was very friendly and cordial. His father had been a good friend of Uncle Cam's. As a little boy, Ambassador Luna had spent some time (about two weeks) at Yarinacocha, at the home of Uncle Cam and Elaine. We can be assured that both of them made that little boy feel at home, and he sensed that he counted with them.

The Townsend children had learned gracious hospitality from their parents, so I'm confident that they made sure he was included in everything. So, that young boy came away with happy memories, and today holds SIL in Peru in high esteem. Little did Uncle Cam and Elaine dream that same little boy would someday become Peru's Ambassador to the United Nations. Then again, that's what Uncle Cam said might happen—that someone we show kindness to today might someday be in a high place. I'm sure Uncle Cam has heard and is smiling to himself. He might even be saying, "I told you so!"

Chapter 30 - Audio Recording of the New Testament

Handwritten Prayer Letter (p. 2)

Thank you for making my trip to Peru possible. You prayed, you gave (thousands of dollars for the Recording Project, thousands more for Gracie and me) time and practical help and gifts to speed me on my way. You expressed love and concern, and more. Thank you. Thank you. I trust you had a blessed holiday season, and that you have a wonderful year ahead.

Handwritten Prayer Letter (p. 7)

It was evident that many prayed for us because although it was a battle all the way, illness on the part of almost everyone involved, even the recordist, operations for two of the Indians, Sinora hemhorraging [*sic*], Arpi rushed to hospital, children sick, bad news from home—Arpi's brother shot at and threatened—personal problems, Manuel ready to quit because of betrayal by a supposed friend—mechanical problems with the equipment, etc., etc. In spite of it all it was a very productive time and wonderful things happened during our time in Peru. I praise God for your faithfulness.

Handwritten Prayer Letter (p. 8)

The recording of the Candoshi-Shapra New Testament (we completed more than half on audio tape) was done very professionally thanks to an excellent recordist, Manuel Pereyra, four good readers, Arpi and his wife Masho; Matarina (daughter of Chief Tariri); and Yodari Máxkina—Sinora's wife, who was illiterate but spoke the women's parts in the Gospels by memorizing them. John Tuggy oversaw the editing and copying of tapes, etc. Gracie oversaw the care of two families, tending to their every need. Sheila oriented Gracie, and helped her with the Indians—also tutoring Sinora and the Candoshi children. John continued reviewing the tapes, etc., after we left for the tribe. He listened to everything at least three times and wrote us, "All the recordings sound great."

Handwritten Prayer Letter (p. 9)

We praise God for the spiritual awakening at Shoroya. I'd almost dreaded going because of the report Arpi and Matárina gave us on the situation there. We could almost feel the darkness and oppression there. We are thankful for the healing of the community at Chigana. We praise God for all the hearts and lives touched by Him in each community we visited.

The Indians want me to come back to record the rest of the Candoshi New Testament. They have asked to have a video of the Jesus Film (Luke) dubbed in Candoshi. They would also like the Genesis video. I'm not sure about the feasibility of all this, though I would love to do it. Pray for wisdom and guidance for John Tuggy and the Peru administration as they consider this.

Handwritten Prayer Letter (p. 10)

I praise the Lord for all of you who prayed, gave, and encouraged me to return to Peru for this project. I know many of you gave sacrificially. Thank you from the bottom of my heart.

You were patient in all the delays. Thank you for not giving up on me. Almost all the delays were completely out of my control—lack of funds, lack of partner, illness for me (viral exhaustion syndrome, walking pneumonia, labyrinthitis (viral infection of the inner ear), Gracie's accident with her horse, equipment orders delayed, faulty equipment, etc., etc. But after a delay of two years, we finally left by the end of November 1993, and I was able to spend nine months in Peru. God is good.

What now? I am back at International Relations at JAARS and my superior, Dr. Pittman, has a long list of projects for me which I won't list now; priority items are writing some chapters to update *Tariri, My Story* (with Ethel Vallis' permission,) writing up some other stories from Peru, transcribing Candoshi texts, and such. For this you will need to get a computer and take a computer course. I couldn't imagine this happening soon, but I signed up for three beginner's courses here in January, and tentatively for an intermediate course, planning to rent a computer for that time. They aren't usually available beyond that time. But a colleague returning overseas was updating his equipment and offered his computer (a 386, but I forget the little-known brand) and printer for sale for $675.00. Our main computer expert here confirmed that it was what I needed for my work—mainly word processing, so I got permission to take that amount out of my retirement funds to buy it. *Pray* I will learn well how to use it. I am totally computer-illiterate.

By the way, my niece Jennifer is in nursing school at Presbyterian Hospital, Charlotte, N.C. Christopher, my nephew, had to drop out of Taylor for financial reasons. He is working in a lawyer's office in New York City. Thanks for praying for that too.

May God, the source of hope, fill you with all joy,

Lorrie Anderson

P.S. If you send any funds to me, or to Wycliffe *for* me (see address below), for a particular purpose, project, or piece of equipment, you must state that. I cannot designate it—that must be done by the donor. If you don't write a letter, I believe you can just enclose a separate note (even a post-it. "Lorrie Anderson—Peru trip." Undesignated funds go toward my support. (Check with H. Kruzan.)

Chapter 32 - I'd Love to See a Wild Indian

The time has come which I dreaded so. One of those unknown fears I had has become known. As we came out, I felt very strongly that we would have things to fear among the Shapras, although I didn't quite know what. I don't know why I felt that way because I had feared neither the Piros, nor the Cashibo.

I just never had any fear of Indian men, because among most tribes they are very respectful to white women, and are usually friendly, but not too much so. They feel protective and want to take care of us. As I've said, the one fear I have along that line is *drunken Indians*. There are few other fears I have in the jungle—I would say almost none— neither "tigers" (jaguars), nor snakes, nor lizards, nor alligators, nor bugs, nor so many other things which are commonly feared.

The way we have seen Satan work to stop the work in all the tribes, keeping people from going, causing them to return before time, etc. has made us know that Satan was not going to leave us alone. He tried very hard to keep us from coming out here and delayed us a great deal. He has attacked spiritually, physically, and mentally.

While I was still at the base waiting to go, I had a series of abscesses under my arm and a bad earache. They both cleared up before I left, but then on the trip another abscess appeared under my arm, and I got an infection in my leg. The abscess broke and went away but I felt another lump coming.

It started with a tiny pimple or infected bite on the back of my leg (the upper calf). We were on the trip from Monday to Saturday, so I could not take care of it very well and it got badly infected. It hurt, so I could hardly walk, and it kept me awake nights. In fact, I have hardly had a good night's sleep since leaving the base almost two weeks ago. It was a bad infection which started in one spot and burst through the skin in four other places. Now there are one large and several small holes in my leg which make it look like a tropical ulcer. I have never seen a worse one—not even on the natives and I've seen some bad ones. It looks like some on the slides missionaries show to horrify people. If it is healing at all, it is healing slowly. When the infection was all inside and red and swollen and paining so much, I thought I had, or would have, blood poisoning. When it became full of pus, and later began to be eaten away, I thought I might have gangrene.

You know the thoughts that go through one's mind at a time like that—especially being out in the middle of the jungle without much to treat it (everything was still packed). We had no walls nor floors on the house yet and no place to put things, so it wasn't practical to unpack until we did. And no radio contact with the doctor when we arrived here because a part of the radio was missing, the transmitter, of all things.

Sometimes I wondered if I'd lose my leg, or even die of blood poisoning. (I really feel now that it was God's grace that I did not.) You can imagine what a nervous strain it was. Usually I don't worry a lot, nor do I hardly ever wake up in the night. But I believe Satan has just been trying to get me down. There have been moments of pain, especially with my leg, and weakness, when I didn't care whether I lived or died. How subtle Satan is. I pray that the Lord will heal my leg and just strengthen me physically in every way.

Oh yes, another thing in connection with this. I wanted to tell you all of this because these are the things that led up to and explain why this scare hit me so hard. It was 'the straw that broke the camel's back.'

When we arrived here at the village and could get at our medicine, we got out what was supposed to be sulfadiazine, to take care of my leg. I took it according to the dosage I'd given to many adults in the tribe, so I am sure the dosage was all right. But we didn't have any baking soda to take along with it, which is supposed to counteract bad reactions. Also, you are supposed to drink lots of water, because I think sulfa reduces body fluids. I forgot this point, and because here it isn't convenient to drink much water (it all needs to be boiled), I didn't.

Then I began to have trouble with dizziness and my eyes 'blurring.' I don't know how to describe how my eyes acted, but I couldn't look at one thing, or person, very long, because my eyes didn't seem to focus well. I was scared to keep taking the medicine, and scared to stop, because my infection was so bad. But then, the day after we had this scare, of which I'm going to tell you, the *patrones* came to visit. The wife of one was chatting as I did dishes, and she saw some pills which I'd kept out because I dropped them on the floor. She asked me what kind they were, and I said, "Sulfadiazine." She seemed amazed and said they were exactly like some "Aralen" tablets they had. There is a "W" on one side, which she says stand for "Winthrop and Co." and "A" on the other side, which she says stands for "Aralen."

I was not surprised, because it came from an old jar of medicine of Doris'. The jar said "Sulfadiazine" but contained these pills and Anacin as well. I've always been very careful about taking medicine, and keeping my bottles well labeled, and throwing away unlabeled bottles of medication. I've heard so much in the States about accidents due to taking medicine you're not sure of.

Even though the bottle was labeled, I said to Doris, "Are you sure this is Sulfadiazine?" She was sure. No doubt, as far as she knew, it was. It was an old bottle we'd had in Miaria, among the Piros, and maybe when Esther gathered up and packed some of the last things we'd left there, she might have dumped several kinds of pills in one bottle. We have a new bottle of sulfadiazine someplace, but it is still packed.

Well, the conclusion of all this chatter about medicine is that I decided that settled it—I would stop taking the pills. So, whether I was taking sulfadiazine and just got bad reactions from the drug itself, or from lack of bicarbonate of soda, and liquids, or whether I was taking Aralen without having malaria, I didn't know. Later on, I found it was Aralen I was taking. Although I got malaria shortly after that, and the Aralen perhaps helped some, I was taking too much Aralen. It affects the eyes and nerves.

Just for the curiosity of it, I'd like to know what would happen if you took Aralen when you thought you were taking sulfadiazine for a leg infection. Aralen is a very specific drug, I understand, only for malaria, and dangerous to take. I started out taking 8 Aralen a day for 2 days and 4 a day for the following days, thinking it was the sulfadiazine. I'd like to ask some doctor or nurse who would know.

Wednesday, August 2, 1950

You won't mind if I continue in green ink, will you? I came to the end of my bottle of blue. I hope there is more blue ink packed away some place, but I haven't come across it yet. We have unpacked only the bare necessities and are living in a very unsettled state from day to day—typical mission style. Our house is being built around us and it will be very nice when it is finished.

Thursday, August 3, 1950

There isn't much time to write letters here in the tribe (as you've heard me say dozens of times before). I worked on the language all yesterday morning and planned to write letters all afternoon. We wouldn't usually plan to take a large chunk out of the day for letters, but this will be our last chance to write letters and get them out for quite a while perhaps. The plane is coming next week, we hope, to take out Señor Gutiérrez, the Peruvian Christian who allocated us and has been directing the Indians in building our house our first week here.

By the time I did dinner dishes yesterday, and we took our baths and washed our clothes, and I wrote the few lines above, it was time for me to make supper. So, that's the way it goes. It surely is true that without native help it takes 99% of a missionary's time just to exist.

Have you ever wished you could see wild Indians right out in the jungle, and have you wondered how you would feel if they came yelling through the woods, spear in hand, and surrounded you? Did you think you'd be scared as they encircled you more closely, some glowering and others laughing and chattering in a language you didn't understand? Did you think you'd be very calm if a witch doctor, his face painted red and donning a colorful headdress came slowly toward you looking grim? I have always wanted to see wild Indians, and wondered how I would react. Well, I got my wish, and I found out.

It was a week ago today. And we had gone back to the little stream in the woods to bathe and wash clothes. I had told Doris how I had lain awake a long time the night before praying for the Shapras, and dreaming of what the future held for them and us. I looked forward to the day when we would have the language all analyzed and in writing, when we'd teach them to read in their own language, and we'd translate the Scriptures into Shapra and they would read it, and we would have the thrill of telling them about the Gospel in their language.

I looked back on the way the Lord had led in laying the Shapras on our hearts and had brought us here after many delays. I was thrilled and filled with joy as I thought of the tribe the Lord has given us and filled us with love for them. When I finally went to sleep it was with determination to see the job to the finish—that of giving the Shapras the Word of God in their own language, no matter what the cost.

I think the Lord brought all of these things to mind to strengthen my resolve, so that I would be prepared to stand against Satan the following day. (The key words, "No matter what the cost.")

We chattered as we came back along the lonely path to our house. I don't recall it now, but Doris tells me she said, "Don't you wish we could see some of those upriver Shapras?" I'm sure I said, "Yes," for that was one of my desires too—to meet them and all the other Shapras and give them the Gospel. Then when all the Shapras have been reached, we hope to go to the Muratos, who are supposed to speak the same language, but they may speak a different dialect, which may mean more work on the language before we can give them the Gospel. We didn't realize how soon we'd get the wish which Doris had just voiced.

As we approached our house, we were surprised to see two Indians standing beside it, for the village had been deserted all day. All the men had gone off to hunt, or work, getting material to build our house. The two men didn't smile, though we smiled. We tried to look friendly because we couldn't say much. No response. So, we went about our business in the house (under our roof, I should say because we had no floor or walls yet). The men continued to regard us suspiciously, wondering, no doubt, why these intruders had come. And we are intruders, for though they were strangers to us, and they do not belong to this village, we had made an entrance into their territory.

Then, as if we didn't have enough to frighten us, there appeared at the top of the hill, where the path comes up from the river, a terrifying sight. Two men were advancing slowly and grimly. I'll never recognize the second man again—I didn't give him a second glance—for my eyes were fastened on the first man. He was dressed like the others, as I recall, but was very old and his face was painted with bright red designs, and he had a crown of red and yellow plumes on his head. He was a colorful picture, and I will always wish we had a picture of him as he came. Everyone, even the gang, seemed hushed in his presence. My first thought as he came toward us was, "This is the climax; here comes the witchdoctor to bewitch us, or carry us off, and no one even within calling distance."

He looked so fierce and hostile, but later proved to be the most harmless, for that day at least. I think we had the presence of mind to say, *Buenas tardes*, although I don't recall. He just looked at us briefly, turned, and stood at a distance. He didn't either encourage or discourage the other fellows in their antics.

We found out later that he was Old Shutka, the chief of the upriver community, and he had come down with this gang of young fellows, many his sons, to sell some rubber-like substance called *goma* to the *patrones*. (I think it was probably *chicle* for chewing gum.) The *patrones* and Señor Gutiérrez later told us that he was not a witchdoctor, but merely a chief and was decked out for the trip.

This may be true, but the Peruvians do not know everything about the Indians, nor do they tell all they know. They've also told us the Indians have no religion, which later we found out to be untrue. They also told us they never get drunk, which we already knew to be false. They have already admitted now that the Indians do drink fermented *masato* and have fiestas and paint up and dance, as well as get drunk and make lots of noise.

The crowd again resumed their chatter, and wandered around looking at our beds, and things (of which there weren't many because we had only unpacked a few things). I sat down on a box, and looked over Shapra words in my notebook, and Doris came and stood alongside. The fellows came and surrounded us again coming closer and closer, but not touching us. Most of them continued to talk and laugh in a most boisterous way—like a whoop, or *yi!* Others stood there silently regarding us and glaring in a belligerent way. One had a stick and kept beating it against his skirt as he kept his eyes fastened on us. It was these latter ones which sent chills down my spine, though the gayer ones made me uncomfortable.

I had been praying, of course, that the Lord would protect us, and help us, but I thought instead of repeating, "Dear Lord, please protect us; please bring Mr. Gutierrez back soon," I might rather pray more constructively. So, I opened my notebook to my daily prayer list and prayed for my family, for you and other friends, for the church, the pastors, Wilsie, my Sunday School teacher, and others.

All of a sudden, the fellows got a sudden inspiration, and with one accord they yelled and whooped and went prancing across the clearing and stampeded up on the platform of the chief's house, next to ours, where all of our boxes and duffel bags were piled. We sighed with relief for we were at least separated by a little distance. I had stopped trembling when I sat down before, but we were still frightened, and wished we could run and hide someplace.

Doris suggested that if they went down the hill out of sight we could run back to the house in the woods where most of the women were. I felt then, and realize now too, that it would have been folly to run from them. It is quite a distance to that house, and they were so fleet-footed. I think too, it might have been a signal for them to bother us more than they had if they had realized how really frightened we were. I think the way we acted was wise (and it was the Lord guiding us, of course), and if they come again (I mean "when"), and if they act the same way, it will be wise for us to respond to their antics with calmness, and quiet dignity, even though we likely will have the same impulse to flee.

We looked up and were further relieved to see Señor Gutiérrez slowly wending his way over the logs. I thought he looked very old, and tired, and seemed almost reluctant to return. I imagine he kind of dreaded it, not knowing what to expect of that crowd of ruffians. We said, "How good you came. We prayed you would. We were frightened." He said he had known they were here, but knowing they wouldn't hurt us had not come immediately. He had been working in the woods not too far away with Miranda and Manuel (a Peruvian, and a Huambisa Indian, who are helping him just until the house is completed).

The ruffians saw that Mr. Gutiérrez had returned, and in typical manner came dashing back, and gathered around to ask him questions about us and why we had come. He speaks a little Shapra since he worked in this area and traded rubber with them about twenty years ago. He explained, as best he could, our motives for coming, and what we were going to do here. I am sure he was nervous, and perhaps even frightened as he conversed with them, for he spoke very slowly and very quietly. He acted quite differently than he ever had before, and his manner was very different than when he dealt with the friendly Indians here.

Suddenly (they do everything this way) their leader, whoever he was, whichever one he was, gave the signal, imperceptible to us, and with more yells and leaps they disappeared into the woods as quickly as they had come. Mr. Gutiérrez assured us again that we were in no danger with those Indians, but I'm not sure he was completely convinced of it himself.

Knowing we were upset, he suggested we go see the bath place he had prepared at the brook in the woods. It is a private place where no one else goes. They had cleared out a place by the brook, and made a rack to hang our clothes and a bench across the brook where we could sit and wash clothes. The three of them had worked on it all day and it was a surprise for us. They had been there all the time, but I think preferred not to appear while the wild crowd was here. Miranda and Manuel hadn't come out of hiding. When I saw how the roughnecks treated these two the next day, I could understand why they tried to avoid them. They were bullies, and because they are in the majority, take advantage of those who aren't. The next day they teased Miranda and Manuel unmercifully, first one, and then the other.

The Shapras are a very proud people—and with reason, for they are fine physical specimens, are intelligent, and have charming personalities. They excel in everything in their jungle world. They just have no respect for the Huambisas, and consider them dirt under their feet. They consider themselves superior to all tribes, and all races, so even Peruvians and Americans don't impress them much. They are "the people" and act accordingly.

I had calmed down while the fellows were still here, so I ate supper as usual with Doris and Señor Gutiérrez, and we talked of the day's events. He continued to assure us that we had nothing to fear. He left shortly and then "it" hit me. What, I'm not sure. At the time I thought it was a nervous reaction from the day's fright. Now, since finding out that I had been taking Aralen when I thought I was taking sulfadiazine, I am sure that had more to do with it. I think that very likely I would have felt the same even if we had never met those Indians, but that surely added to it. I felt so nervous and jittery, hot and cold, nauseated, and had a backache. At one point I thought I was going to faint. Doris let me sleep in her bed.

I stayed awake a long time. I just felt that it was an attack of Satan, for on every hand as we've tried to come to this tribe, and as we've been here, he had tried to disrupt. I surely was upset that night and felt nearer to a nervous breakdown than ever before in my life. In fact, I never have felt like a nervous breakdown before. I've always considered my nerves very steady. But the tropics surely do affect your nerves. I've always had such pride in my calmness and emotional stability. But we have no right to have pride about anything. The Lord needs to teach us lessons the hard way sometimes though I feel this was an attack of Satan, yet the Lord taught me a lesson through it—one of complete dependence upon Him.

I really felt at the end of myself. I wanted to run as far away as I could, and yet I couldn't bear the thought of leaving these precious Indians. What I was afraid of more than anything else, was that I would have to be sick in bed here, and that's drastic among these Indians, or that I would break down in front of them. I was especially afraid that when the ruffians arrived the next day I would tremble at their presence, and maybe break down and cry in front of them. The Holy Spirit brought verses to my mind, and the most comforting was I Cor. 10:13. Having felt this was an attack of Satan, I pled the Blood of Jesus against his power. After a while the Lord gave me peace and I slept.

Doris didn't have any reaction that day, but the next afternoon she was hysterical—laughing and crying—and we had to go for a walk in the woods until she recovered. She thought it must be something else, but I imagine it was just delayed reaction to our scare. It was a nervous strain for both of us.

The next morning, when I got up, I felt shaky, but soon calmed down and felt fine all day. When the crowd came again, they acted pretty much the same but there were others around. As Doris says, "They decided to give us the scare treatment again." But I didn't tremble, or shake, or break down. I felt quite calm, and my feeling toward them was entirely different. The night before I would have said, "Yes, I love them because they're Shapras, and I hope we can take them the Gospel someday." The next day they gathered around us, and chattered, and laughed, and hoped we were scared. I think they knew we were at least somewhat scared both days and delighted in rubbing it in. But the second day my heart was filled with love for them and a desire for each one individually to come to the Lord.

The reason we don't dare get sick in bed is that these Indians are deathly afraid of sickness and disease, especially the grippe and colds. They were once a large tribe of 10,000 or so, and some white men came in bringing the grippe, measles, or some such, and the Indians died in droves. One of the first questions the village people here asked about us was, "Do they have any diseases?" and the ruffians asked Mr. Gutiérrez the same question. He said, "No, they're in good health," and in general we are.

I certainly have been sick a lot here. But I haven't had to spend a day in bed yet. Yesterday I was sick and had to lie down a little. I don't know what's wrong, but it scares me. I had headache, backache, chills, and fever for the last two nights and yesterday. I still feel weak and dizzy today. That is, no doubt, partly from the hemorrhaging I am experiencing. It's scary. I'm telling you all the gruesome details merely so you know how to pray. Do you have any idea what it could be? [It turned out to be cerebral malaria (*Falciparum*) plus complications of "blackwater fever," a usually fatal disease which occasionally accompanies attacks of malaria of malignant strains.]

Lorrie Doris Anderson,
Letter of July 28, 1950

Chapter 33 - Let the Little Children Come to Me

By Lorrie Anderson

I sat at my desk studying and John Tuggy (one of my co-workers among the Shapra Indians of Peru) came rushing to the door. "I just talked to Tariri," he said. I looked at him blankly. Chief Tariri is four hundred miles north of here near the border of Ecuador. The only radio for hundreds of miles around was the one we had left there, and he would not know how to put that together. But apparently, he did, and he told us that his seven-month-old baby boy was dying of flu. "Send Monchanki and, if the baby dies, we'll cry together," he said.

Our jungle base doctor prescribed medicine and told us how to administer it. We passed the word on to Tariri and told him how to break into our medicine cabinet. Since it was late afternoon, we told him that, if the baby had not improved by morning, we would come.

The director gave permission for the trip and, while the plane was kept standing by, he made telephone calls and did a lot of figuring to see how it could be financed. The doctor filled a little black bag with medicines we might need. Eunice Pike, a visiting linguist and nurse from the Mazatec tribe of Mexico, was released for several days from her duties as consultant and lecturer in the workshop.

The next morning, Tariri reported by radio that the baby, unable to retain the medicine, was worse. "Please come right away; my baby is dying," he said.

After four hours of flying and one hour "gassing up" along the way, we landed on the Morona River at the mouth of the Pushaga. A dugout canoe was waiting for us, and after an hour of travel we arrived at the path. Half an hour of running and walking through the jungle brought us to Tariri's clearing.

Tariri, long hair tousled and eyes red and swollen, met us. Irina, who had not slept for five nights, was stretched out near the oldest daughter, Mayanchi, who was holding the baby. He was a cute, roly-poly baby, and, except for the look in his eyes, he didn't appear seriously ill. But, as we drew near and heard his labored breathing, we knew he was sick and miserable. His temperature was 105.4. They said his fever had lasted for six days, coupled with dysentery and vomiting. Doc had said that one of the main dangers was dehydration. So, after hanging the bottle of fluid from the rafters of the grass-roofed house, Eunice inserted the needle of the tube into the fat little thigh. The Indians were wary of the "new-fangled contraption," but they took our word for it that it was necessary. Eunice, a nurse, sponged him off to reduce his temperature. Then, at intervals, she administered teaspoons of boiled water which they had already prepared for him. (We were glad to see that some of the things we've taught them over the years have sunk in.)

Finally, around eight p.m. we found a few minutes to eat the *yucca* (potato-like tuber) and chicken they had prepared for us. Eunice suggested that we go to bed so that we might get up again at four o'clock. We still had to put up our mosquito nets. Eunice had already settled, and I had my air mattress half blown up when I decided to go over to Tariri's for some lukewarm boiled water to quench my thirst.

Tariri called and said, "His feet are getting cold." I went in and found that they were. His breathing was louder and faster. Though there seemed to be little hope, I thought, "Surely the Lord will spare him." We have seen babies and adults in an apparently worse condition restored to health. In each case we felt that the recovery was miraculous, and I knew that, if the Lord should so choose, He could heal this little baby even at this zero hour. However, in addition to the other lessons the Lord wished the Indians to learn, this experience showed that our presence does not guarantee a miracle.

After a while, Mayanchi, holding the baby, said, "He's dying." The Indians were beginning the high-pitched keening (the death wail). His breathing stopped. His weakened pulse also stopped. Then the wailing began in earnest. It is a shrill, sobbing chant which echoes through the woods and sends chills up and down your spine and rends your heart. "My baby, my baby, you died. I won't see you tomorrow. My baby, my baby, here is the little hammock where you used to sleep." These words were all chanted and sobbed to the same high-pitched tune.

All night long they alternately held the baby and laid him in his hammock. "My brother, my brother," wailed Mayanchi and the other five children. When Irina wasn't holding the baby, she was crying on Tariri's shoulder, or Mayanchi's, or mine. Sometimes they gathered all the children around and hugged them and cried.

The first wails had alerted the settlement, and people came from far and near to join the mourning, and add to the din. I have never seen such mourning for a baby and though it seemed to be the most heathen mourning I had ever seen, yet the atmosphere, that would have seemed so noisy and unruly to an outsider, was really different. There was a quietness in the midst of the wailing. There was no raving nor bitterness. Even though Tariri and Irina wailed and refused to be comforted at first, they never once said, as in the old days before they knew Christ, "Why did this happen to me? God hates me!" The sympathy shown by the others was wonderful to see. Tariri once was hated and feared, even by most of his own group, and he was followed only as a leader in war. But now he is loved and respected, even by those who refused to follow his Christ, and by those who chided him for not following the tribal code of killing for revenge.

Matárina and Arosa, two of Tariri's littlest girls, each asked me separately, "Did he die?" "Yes, he died," I said talking directly into their ears to overcome the din, "but you'll see him again someday in heaven. He's in God's house now. Mommy and Daddy are crying because they didn't want the baby to go away. But we don't need to cry for the baby. He'll never be sick or hurt or cry again. God is taking care of him." I could tell from their eyes, and from Matárina's smile, that they were satisfied. Oh, that we would all be as little children!

It was about 2 o'clock in the morning when I succeed in getting everyone quieted and seated. I told the story (as Eunice had suggested) of David, the great chief of Old Testament times ("before Jesus was born") who cried and mourned while his child was sick, but when the child died, David stopped mourning. He said: *But now he is dead; Wherefore should I fast? Can I bring him back again? I shall go to him, but he shall not return to me* (II Samuel 12:23). I explained to the chief and his family, "David believed that he would see his baby again. You will see your baby again in heaven because you know the Lord." That settled them for a while. I gave a sedative to Irina, and she put the baby back in his hammock. They permitted me to put up their muslin sleeping tent for protection from malaria mosquitos and vampire bats; then they lay down and were quiet.

The next morning, at our early morning radio contact, we told the base that the baby had died, and that we would be returning. The radio operator asked whether we would like someone to talk to Tariri. Our director, ready to catch a plane for Lima at nearby Pucallpa, gladly took time to speak at length to Tariri words of comfort which I translated into the Shapra tongue. John Tuggy, Beth Hinson, and Shiniki Kasímoró, who was at the base for a teacher training course, also radioed words of sympathy which Tariri gratefully received.

Early on that same morning, Tariri's brother had gone to the woods to carve out a little canoe from balsa wood. With it he brought back a large piece of bark for a covering. Other men were mending the roof of the hut nearby where the body of the baby would be left. The body, together with a few of his little belongings, would be placed inside the canoe which was raised on forked sticks, covered with the bark, and protected by the thatched roof. A fire burning under the canoe would keep bugs and worms away, they said. When only the bones are left, they will be put into a clay pot and placed high on a shelf in the chief's house. (Keeping the bones does not seem to involve any reverence of them—they get no more attention, except that the mother will cry over them from time to time.)

Irina and Tariri were wrapping the little body in the best material they had. We had hoped for an early "burial" so that we could have a little funeral service. We told the family that we were sorry to have to leave at this point, but the plane was needed back at the base, and the pilot had told us we must leave at least by noon if we were to reach the base the same day. I suggested that we read a portion of scripture and have prayer before they finished preparing the body for "burial." From a mimeographed copy of the Gospel of Mark in Shapra, chapter 10, verses 13 through 16, we read how little children were brought to Jesus while he was teaching. The disciples said: *Don't bother the Master*. But Jesus said, *Let the children come to me; do not hinder them, for to such belongs the Kingdom of God.* After prayer, they quietly continued their preparations while I spoke a few words of farewell to each person, last of all to Tariri and his family. It was hard to tear ourselves away when they were still in need of fellowship and comfort. Tariri said, "If you would stay five days with us, we might not mind letting you go."

By the end of the trip both Eunice and I had been impressed with one thing: how wonderful it is to be a member of this team. I was touched by the loving, prayerful interest shown by everyone who had anything to do with the trip—the director, the doctor, the flight coordinator, the pilot, the radiomen, and all the others. To them it was not merely another job to be done; it was not even only a matter of saving the life of one baby; it was, instead, a determination that everything possible should be done to assist in giving the Word of God to a tribe. Everyone was working toward that one purpose. Many times since, I have praised the Lord for the privilege of being a member of this team.

Chapter 34 - Finally: The Scriptures In Print

Lorrie - December 17, 2011

LAT Prayer and Praise
December 10, 2010

Praise. Wednesday, Dr. Honeycutt examined me thoroughly since I've had a cold since October 8. He concluded my lungs and breathing are normal with no congestion, though I often cough at night. I told him what would be involved in the roundabout, and difficult travel, to the Candoshi-Shapra Scripture dedication in the jungles of Peru. He has reservations about my going, but did not want to tell me not to go. Judy Boyd had wanted for a long time to go with me to our dedication, but did have reservations about the trip. She had a phone chat with John Tuggy, just back from Peru (part of our translation team with his wife Sheila—they translated all the Old Testament books, as well as a good part of the New Testament).

She's going to call me, and I'm anxious to know what John's advice is, since he told the Shapra Chief at Shoroya that I would be coming down for the celebration. I'm anxious to hear what he has to say now. My niece had reservations about it, and I'm sure S.I.L. does too, but Todd, my physical therapist, is enthusiastic, and cheering me on. There is one possibility that would make for a relatively "easy" trip, if SAMAIR would be willing and able to take us "directly" to the jungle town of San Lorenzo. Please pray for God's clear guidance for me.

Prayer. Arpi is in Yurimaguas to look at DVD players and buy a good quality one. (We've had donations for one from a Peru/JAARS couple, a Greensboro friend, and an old friend of High School days, which will cover most of it.) I'd been excited that it is looking like Arpi will finally get to go upriver to backslider Tskimbo Bisa's home to show the whole film *Life of Christ* in the Candoshi-Shapra language, to him and his family, along with daily Bible studies, but alas! there is another delay. Arpi has looked all over Yurimaguas and can only find inferior unknown brands. We were excited when he found a Sony with a nice large screen, but when he went back with the DVD to test it, it turned out to be a used one that did not function properly. Pray God will guide him to the right city later upon his return—none of them are close by. So as of now he will just go to Tskimbo Bisa's and teach the Word daily for a week, and fellowship with them. Tskimbo has told Arpi he was really looking forward to an extended time for them to fellowship together in the Lord. Pray there will be no further delay.

LAT Prayer and Praise
February 4, 2011

I continue to praise the Lord for His blessing in letting me go to Peru for the dedication of the new volume of Scripture in Candoshi-Shapra (key passages of the Old Testament, 40%, and the whole New Testament.) It was good to see many of the Shapras there, and some Candoshis (who live farther away), the leaders in the full regalia of the old days, addressing the crowd about what it meant to them to have this volume of Scripture. Pray that those who bought the Book will read it daily, and have their lives changed by God's living Word, and that it will be possible to get it distributed soon to the scattered several thousand who were not there. It was good to see Tskimbo Bisa, who has recently turned his life around, interpreting for the Spanish visitors—Peru Bible Society, pastors from the Moyobamba Presbyterian Church, etc. I praise God for all He did to make it possible for me to go—Dan Hudson who accompanied me, those who gave financial gifts, etc. Thank you for your faithful prayers.

I was glad for special guests, Josh Kitchen, new WBT member. Also, for Raphael Baylor, Swiss Indian Mission, who will soon move to a Candoshi or Shapra community, with his wife and 2 little children, to minister to them. This is a special joy to me because I was very fond of his parents, Heinz and Petronella, who were missionaries to the people there when the Tuggys and I had to leave after the dedication of the New Testament in 1980. His parents learned the language well and dearly loved the Indians. The Indians loved them in return, and were very sad when Heinz came down with Hepatitis B and they had to return to Switzerland. I was able to talk to Raphael, on the lone tribal cell phone this week, as he visited Shoroya. He is visiting as many communities as possible looking for God's spot for them. Pray for clear guidance for them. He told of visiting the villages on the Xapuri River in the Candoshi area near Lago Rimachi—all 18 of them. (When we visited them years ago there were only three, as I recall!)

Among the many visitors who came to chat with me in my hostel quarters were Vahacha, his wife Irina, and their chubby, healthy twins. Thanks for all your prayers for them. I had a good chat with Tskimbo, among others. He said he and Yámpisa are both serious about renewing their walk with the Lord. He is waiting anxiously for Arpi to come for a week of teaching and fellowship. There is another delay with the oil company having called for Shapra men to come to Shoroya. Tskimbo should be arriving there tomorrow. Chief Masorashi and teacher Chiriapa are concerned that the *mestizos/petroleros* who work with the company will bring diseases from the outside to their community. Pray that when these workshops are over, and Tskimbo leaves for home, that Arpi will be able to go with him for a week's visit as planned. Pray that if these delays are of Satan, that Arpi will be strong, and not allow anything to further deter him from what God desires.

LAT Prayer and Praise
February 11, 2011

Another delightful time on the Peru trip for which I praise the Lord: The only feasible way for me to get to San Lorenzo for the dedication was by chartering a SAMAIR plane from Pucallpa (a large jungle city near Yarinacocha). Craig Gehagan, pilot, said we should come stay overnight at their house so we could leave first thing in the morning. Heather Gehagan fixed a delicious dinner, and invited friends over. Heather asked if I would tell the story of the anaconda attack. I don't enjoy telling it, but they said they were blessed by hearing of God's intervention.

I'd been homesick for Peru, and flying over miles of jungle and winding rivers, the next morning, and the following day, was a joy. Craig is an excellent pilot, and I have perfect confidence in him, as I do in the JAARS pilots. The flight was smooth, so it was very relaxing. I praise the Lord for this special treat. I am thankful also that Craig offered to stay overnight in San Lorenzo after the dedication, so I could have time to fellowship with as many of the Indians as possible.

This morning we had 10 people at my house to bid farewell to, and pray for, Ron and Michelle Smith, and children. They are with *Perú en fuego* (I think he's the president.) I met them last week when her mother asked me to take part with Michelle and their 3 teenage children in a 3-

hour Q and A time for several of the grade school classes at W.C.A. It was lively, and when Michelle and I were able to talk, I was impressed with the heart she has for the unreached.

They live in, and work out of, Lima, but they go up into the mountains, and out into the jungle. They want to get more involved, and work with them more in depth. (Special friends are the Nystroms and the Keagys. Michelle meets weekly for prayer with Karen.) Their prayer is that they will know more of God's heart, and be able to work more in depth with the people.

Please keep praying for Arpi, for a wife, for guidance concerning Bible school (we found out there are 3 courses, 2 with South America Mission—one short—as well as the one with Swiss Indian Mission) and for his ministry. Arpi and Tskimbo are still trying to get together for a week of in-depth teaching, along with the *Life of Christ* DVD. Please pray for victory over Satan, if he is the one throwing a monkey wrench into their plans at every attempt to follow through on something definite. Right now, Tskimbo is downriver again.

LAT Prayer and Praise
April 29, 2011

Praise. I am rejoicing that Raphael Baylor and his wife have arrived to settle in one of the Candoshi, or Shapra, communities to minister to them—encouraging the unsaved to trust Christ, and challenging the believers to live in such a way that others cannot resist His call. Right now, they are spending several weeks at Shoroya where Arpi, his family, Chief Tariri's children and grandchildren live, along with lots of newcomers. I don't know where they have decided to settle, and have not been able to contact him. He is staying at the far end of the village, and when I asked if he might come to the phone, they said he'd gone out in the jungle with some of the men. I'm anxious to find out where they plan to settle, and be able also to ask him questions about the Bible school that Arpi would like to attend.

You may remember that I met Raphael—for the first time since he grew up—at the Candoshi-Shapra new "Bible" dedication in January. I was thrilled to know he had the vision to commit himself and his family to work among the Candoshi-Shapras. I also told you how I greatly admired his parents, Heinz and Petronella, who lived among the people for several years until he came down with Hepatitis B, and was told by the doctor his only hope was to return to Switzerland. They spoke the language well, and were dearly loved by the people, so it was heartbreaking all around. Praise the Lord for the vision God has given this young couple (they have a five-year-old boy and a little two-year-old girl.)

Please keep praying for Arpi. I have not been able to get him for over a week. He has found some ways to make money (which is very rare out there). He and his son have been working on getting some lumber—enormous trees—to float downriver, and sell. Today he'd gone to help a man who is making a large dugout canoe. Pray Arpi may get his new DVD-TV equipment fixed in the far distant city, so he can go minister to Tskimbo and family who await the showing of the *Life of Christ* video at their home upriver.

Epilogue

It has been a joy to share with you about God's work among the Shapra people. And God is still at work through believers like Masorashi and others who love the Lord. I thank the Lord for Doris Cox. By God's grace, Doris and I had different gifts. Doris was a better linguist; I was better at relating to the people. Rachel Saint spent a short time with us at the very first. And, of course, there were John and Sheila Tuggy who came along a little later and did most of the actual translation. But it was, and is, God's work through frail vessels.

I pray every day for the progress of the Gospel among the people, that the history of how the Lord touched Tariri's heart early on, and changed him from a killer to a godly leader, will continue to be used to bring more and more to Jesus as Lord.

Please pray with me that the Holy Spirit will work mightily among the Candoshi and the Shapra, to the glory of God.

Lorrie Doris Anderson

****

Acknowledgements:
My beloved niece Jennifer Langford has been my delight and has cared for me in these latter years. My cousin John Flood and his wife Doris have been crucial in putting this memoir together, with help from Newton Frank, Kay McLain and Missy Hicks. Typists Emily Smith and Madelyn Beck were most appreciated. There are more friends than could possibly be mentioned who have had a part in my life both during and since the Peru years. And my home church, Hawthorne Gospel Chapel in New Jersey, has upheld me in multiple ways. How I thank God for each and every one.

<u>**Further acknowledgements:**</u>

Chapter 3 - Eppie Richbourg, special writer, Wycliffe Bible Translators (WBT)

Chapter 10 - Grace Watkins (WBT)

Chapter 12 - Richard Pittman (WBT)

Chapter 14 - Robert Griffin (WBT)

Chapter 26 - (WBT) Radio Script #98 B-14

Lorrie's Journal Entries

Journal Entry (pp. 1-5)
January 1956 - Yarinacocha
Didn't have this book with me at Pushaga (I mean with the Shapras), and so, didn't get to write down the many verses the Lord gave me and the blessings. I'll have to go back and list them all later. Right now, I wanted to write down a verse or two the Lord brought me concerning the five martyrs in Ecuador.

On Jan. 10 It fell open to Jeremiah 31 and my eye lighted on vs. 16: *Thus says the Lord Keep your voice from weeping, and your eyes from tears; for your work shall be rewarded, says the Lord, and they shall come back from the land of the enemy."* I hoped it was a promise that the remaining three were still alive, but had no assurance it was. Nevertheless, I gave it to Luke to give Rachel over the radio. It seemed strange that I should find it without looking for it and that it should be stated the way it was—especially since the name *Auca* means "enemy." We know now that it was not a promise for those five—perhaps for later ones. But the middle sentence remains a wonderful promise for Rachel and Marge and the other wives that their efforts on behalf of the Aucas and the efforts of the valiant five were not in vain but will still bear fruit.

This morning I was reading in Esther, and I think the attitude of the five must have been the same as hers when she decided to go plead for her people before the king that they be not destroyed. Though it might mean death for her, she saw no alternative but to go, and she said in 4:16: *Then I will go to the king, though it is against the law; and if I perish, I perish.*

Saturday, February 25ᵗʰ, 1956
For morning devotions, I have been reading portions of Philippians, with Calvin's commentaries on them [this book belongs to Al Townsend]. It has been very thought-provoking, and I wish I'd been writing down each day of the particular blessing. In Philippians 1:17, he says concerning the words "for the defense of the Gospel:" *For since Christ confers upon us so great an honor, what excuse shall we have, if we shall be traitors to his cause or what may we expect, if we betray it by our silence, but that He shall in return desert our cause, who is our*

sole Advocate, or Patron, with the Father? Something I never thought of. That was from the other day. In Philippians 1:19… he tells…beforehand… solitary… not speaking of the safety of the body (whence… It is from what he teaches elsewhere (Romans 8:28))—that all things contribute to the advantage of God's true worshippers, even though the whole world, with the devil its prince, should conspire together for their ruin. In verse 19, on the words "and the supply"—so that the supply of the Spirit is the efficient cause.

Journal Entry (pp. 16-17)
??, 1956

…impressed me especially in the B. version was in verse 20 speaking of repenting and turning to God, … "practice activities consistent with repentance." And verse 28, I think it was in the margin: *You think by a shortcut to make me a Christian.* Later in the day, in Time magazine were two thought-provoking items worthy of putting down for future reference. The following saying is attributed to Peter Marshall, Chaplain of the Senate, and a prayer he prayed there one day. However, his wife is not sure it is original with him. *When we are wrong, make us easy to change. When we are right, make us easy to live with.* The other thought, which Adlai Stevenson [the presidential candidate] sent out on a card acknowledging Christmas cards sent to him. It is by an unknown confederate soldier:

I asked God for strength, that I might achieve,
I was made weak, that I might learn humbly to obey.
I asked for health, that I might do greater things,
I was given infirmity, that I might do better things.
I asked for riches, that I might be happy,
I was given poverty, that I might be wise.
I asked for power, that I might have the praise of men,
I was given weakness, that I might feel the need of God.
I asked for all things, that I might enjoy life,
I was given life, that I might enjoy all things.
I got nothing that I asked for—but everything that I had hoped for,
Almost despite myself, my unspoken prayers were answered.
I am among all men, most richly blessed.

Journal Entries (pp. 18-19)
Monday, March 5th, 1956

I have been especially burdened these days for Señor Beltrán. Tariri gave a good testimony to him and his editorial staff—in fact, the best while he was in Lima. His son was so taken by Tariri that he talked and talked to him and finally gave him a ring [his own?] In these trying days, I trust their thoughts will turn to the simple testimony that Tariri gave, and that they will do much thinking. Yesterday, as I read that poem, I thought especially of the older man. Just now he has the very opposite of all he asked for, but perhaps it is the very best thing for him. Perhaps it is the only thing which would bring him in humility to accept Christ as his Savior.

I'm thankful now for the time in Lima with Tariri (though it was hectic at the time and was even harmful to him in some ways) and for the privilege of meeting the President and other leading figures, because it has given me more of an interest in the Peruvian people and the welfare of the country as a whole. Now they are no longer just names to me, but people I should have an interest in and pray for, but having met some, they are now people [human beings] to me and I'm burdened for them as such. Read Acts 27 in the R.S.V. I like the phrase in verse 23: *The God to whom I belong and whom I worship.*

Friday, March 9th, 1956

Read Romans 2. Thought of verses 1-11, especially in connection with Señor Beltrán, and do pray that somehow the Word *will* reach him that he may meditate upon it and see his needs. Verse 13 is a reminder: *The doers of the law*, and…

Journal Entry (pp. 22-23)

…to translate for the Shapras at this time. After the broadcast and dishes, I read Acts 8 and Psalms 30 and 31. As a special promise, the Lord gave me Psalm 30:5: *For His anger is but for a moment, and His favor is for a lifetime. Weeping my tarry for the night, but joy comes with the morning.* Verses 11 and 12 are good too. Verse 9 of Psalm 31 expressed the way I feel today, but I'm not in as bad a state, fortunately, as the verses following down to verse 13.

Verses 14 and 15: *But I trust in Thee, O Lord, I say 'Thou art my God.' My times are in Thy hand.*

Verse 19: *O how abundant is Thy goodness, which Thou hast laid up for those who fear Thee, and wrought for those who take refuge in Thee,* to the end of verse 20. And again, at the end, a promise and challenge: *Love the Lord, all you His saints! The Lord preserves the faithful, but abundantly requites him who acts haughtily. Be strong, and let your heart take courage, all you who wait for the Lord!*

Journal Entry (pp. 24-25)

Later—On an IVCF Intercessor folder, another verse that blesses: *When my soul fainted within me,* **I remembered the Lord***: and my prayer came in unto Thee, into Thine holy temple.* Jonah 2:7.

Tuesday, October 18th, 1956 [Doris' birthday - 4/3/2012]

Doris was on the air this morning and able to tell me a few more details. The baby who was accidently shot in the fray was Arosa's and Chiriapa's darling Toripi. He was one of my favorite babies—sweet and good-natured and so cute. She just recently had a miscarriage, and now that leaves her only little Wautista, who isn't well, and may not live to grow up. She may have none of Chiriapa's children left to remember him by. My heart goes out to her—her husband and baby killed in one day, and at the hand of her father, and brothers. It was old Shutka who came down with his sons Pirocha and Pinchu, to kill his son-in-law Chiriapa and his grandson Toripi. They arrived and Tariri thought it was a friendly visit [even though they had not blown their horn] and invited them to come in…

Journal Entry (pp. 26-27)

…to sit down. He sat down, and—suddenly realizing it was not a friendly visit—he jumped up. Pinchu shot Chiriapa and Pirocha shot Tariri.

How they could do this to their own sister's husband, and their own uncle [Tariri], I don't know. And what reason they gave in their own hearts, I don't know. That's what hurts so much. It's bad enough to have someone you love killed, but to have him killed by others you love, doubles the sorrow. To think that they, especially Pinchu, who professes [salvation] could care so little, not only for Chiriapa and Tariri, but for us, and the Gospel, is crushing. I still feel that [his mother] Inchi is the main one behind it all (of course, and she is the devil's pawn.)

But what about Pinchu? Is he a believer who just finds all the pressure of the culture, and the pressure of his family too much to buck against—or is he not a believer after all? I still want to believe he may be. But I don't see how a believer can continue in killing like that, and yet...

Journal Entry (pp. 28-29)

...maybe I did not know then that there were rumors that Arosa's other brother (and Chiriapa) had killed Shutka's oldest sons (teenagers).

We do not know what goes on in their minds, or how strong the pressure of the culture pattern must be. Yet in this killing I cannot see how they could justify their actions, even to themselves. What reasons could they possibly give? (*Reasons out of Inchi's maniacal imagination?*) Perhaps! Oh, Lord, if Pinchu is [Yours?], yet bring him out of that life. Somehow give him the courage even to come down and say "Kill me if you will, to revenge Chiriapa's death, but I could not stay away. I must have what you have. I must have the Lord, or die. I'm tired of the killing and running." O, Lord, yet bring him back to us peacefully.

I'm glad my son, Yámpisa (a close relative of Chief Shutka's) was not in the crowd. He's plenty old enough. I trust it was because he wanted no part of it. He may have begged off saying he had no gun, or his mother may have pled that he does not go, and perhaps be killed.

Journal Entry (pp. 30-31)

Who knows what I might have done, or at least thought if my two precious teenage sons—so handsome, so smart, so everything a young Shapra was expected to be? Maybe I did not know at the time of writing this, in October 1955, that there had been rumors that Irina and Chiriapa's other brothers had unexpectedly run into Shutka and Inchi's two teenage sons hunting in the jungle far from home and killed them.

That could explain why they killed Chiriapa in revenge, since his brothers, the real perpetrators were not readily accessible. Why was Pinchu chosen to be the one to shoot his mild-mannered, loving brother-in-law Chiriapa? Was it because they wanted to cure him once and for all, of all this foolishness of believing in (following?) Jesus? (It was he who shot Sinta or Ankocha).

How can Yámpisa hobnob with those who killed his father and uncle, when he was a child? Does he feel they were justified?

Was it because, since he (Chiriapa) was Arosa's husband, they wanted the most neutral person to shoot him? Maybe her father and her full brothers did not want her pointing her finger at them for having fired the actual shot? (Then again, women and their preferences do not count for much to the Shapras.)

Then, why not the younger Chiriapa? Perhaps they intend to give her to him eventually. I trust the Lord will prevent that. That would be miserable for both Marashu and Arosa and the sister. I trust that in time the Lord will supply His own choice of a new husband for Arosa, and that both will be believers.

Doris says Tariri's recovering (at Yarinacocha, our jungle base), is in the little room under the Wacker's house, where the Smiths live (at present) there while the Wackers are away, so they will be back to keep watch on him…

Journal Entry (pp. 32-33)

…in bed. (She says he has to stay in bed while being treated for gunshot wounds.) I think it was Luke who said the bullet went thru his chest, piercing his lung, but the doctor thinks he has a good chance to pull through. I guess it's more serious than the impression that Don Smith (the pilot) gave by air yesterday.

Luke said the Indians are all down on the little lake off the Morona, about 5 min. by air, south of the Pushaga River.

Doris says Mbisa, Simu, and Sinora have gone to Minaki's (Peruvian witch doctor, friend of Shimbotha's) but she thinks they intend to come back and join the others. Everyone is sticking together she says. That's something to praise the Lord for.

Oh, what a shame for everyone to have to leave behind their new houses and new *chacras*, our fairly new house and the chief's own garden, orchard and all the rest.

Whatever will the poor people eat these days—*so* far from any *chacras*—several days' journey perhaps.

Journal Entry (pp. 34-35)

…reading in RSV) were good. *Therefore, let everyone who is godly offer prayer to Thee; at a time of distress, in the rush of great waters they shall not reach him. Thou art a hiding place for me, Thou preserves me from trouble; Thou dost encompass me with deliverance* (Psalm 32:6-7).

Then the promise to my anxiety at where we and all of them should live—whether we should go back to our houses, whether to settle on the lake (where the land is low and swampy—not good for *chacras* [large gardens] and probably unhealthy and mosquito-ridden) or whether to settle on the lower Pushaga, where Tariri was thinking of settling. This is the promise, *I will instruct you and teach you the way you should go; I will counsel you with my eye upon you.* (vs. 8). Verses 10 and 11 are good too.

I've been reading over today the things in the front of this book from Amy Carmichael—just glancing over and they've been a blessing too.

Journal Entry (pp. 36-37)

Wednesday, October 18, 1956
Didn't talk to Doris this morning and nothing new on the news.

Read Psalm 33, and it starts off with praise. We are to praise the Lord *for* everything, some say. Are we really to praise the Lord for everything? Some things are the work of Satan. How can we praise for those things? I can praise the Lord *in* everything. There is much to praise the Lord for in even this heartbreaking situation.

We can praise the Lord that Chiriapa belonged to Him. We can praise the Lord that the first report was not true and Shiniki and Tsirimpo are still alive. We can praise the Lord that Tariri was not killed by the shot, and that he is improving. I cannot praise the Lord that Chiriapa was killed. If he had just died, then I could be more sure the Lord took Him. Even though it would still be hard on Arosa, their children, his three other children, and Irina—I know the…

Journal Entry (pp. 38-39)

…Lord could have a purpose in it. But this killing seemed so unnecessary. What was their reason for it? It took a life, bereaved a large number of people, and further bloodied the hands of these men—one a believer. Yet I know it was not completely out of the Lord's hands. *He is still sovereign.* Yet we can limit Him, by our unbelief or by sin, and let Satan gain the victory in a situation. Chiriapa was the Lord's, and his life was in His hands. He could not be taken without the Lord's permission. Is it not true that the Lord allows certain things because we have limited Him, and would not have His perfect will?

I cannot praise the Lord that the upriver crowd killed someone else. That Pinchu did. That it was someone of their own group. Could it possibly be the Lord's will that Pinchu…

Journal Entry (pp. 40-41)

…should kill someone? Is it ever the Lord's will that a believer should sin? Rather I would think this situation is the work of Satan and not the Lord's. We have free will and we insist on our will.

This chapter brought out the Sovereignty of God again. Verse 10 is good, also verses 18 and 19.

The verses which stood out today are verses 20 and 21: *Our soul waits for the Lord. He is our help and shield. Yea, our heart is glad in Him, because we trust in His holy name.* It struck me as I read verse 20 that the keynote of the Lord's message to me in these days is *wait! Wait on me.*

This I do know: Whether this situation is the work of Satan or the direct work of the Lord, He will triumph in the end.

Read through everything by Amy Carmichael in the first pages of this notebook, and it has a message for these days: "The house in the storm." He…

Journal Entry (pp. 42-43)

…didn't tell us to build out of reach of the floods, but He told us to build a strong house.

"The beast—victorious—*but only for a little while*" struck me again with force. Satan is triumphant and seems to be laughing at us—*but only for a little while.* God will be triumphant in the end…leaving what we do not know to the Love that has led us all our life long."

"…in acceptance with peace." Though I find it hard to accept Chiriapa's death (from the Journal of October of 1955 killings.) page 43 of Chapters on shooting of Chief Tariri and killing of his brother-in-law, Chiriapa, <u>Yachña</u>, and Pinchu killing him. There is nothing else to do now. It is done, and all the fretting and grieving, will not change it. The only wise thing to do is to accept it, and to let it be a challenge to be more faithful, especially to pray more faithfully for these believers, and unbelievers, and to be more diligent in getting the Word to them quickly.

It is a challenge to a more holy life; that nothing in me may hinder, or cause me to stumble, or to allow Satan to gain the victory. "If we wait a little…

Journal Entry (pp. 44-45)

…while, clarity will be given. Something will tell us. Rather, someone will tell us. The sheep know the Shepherd's voice. The loving thoughts of God direct and perfect all that concern us."

Thursday, October 20ᵗʰ, 1956

Talked to Doris [She's at the base]. Where was I? Was I out with Jeannie at the Agurue's when this happened? I must have been. [Where else?] On the radio and she told me a little more though she still does not know all the details herself. They will have to wait until Tariri is better. She doesn't want to bother him with it now, naturally. He is a little better today but had a bad day Tuesday. He was worried about everything and going on and on. He was more himself yesterday, she said. She said she thinks Irina needs prayer more than anyone, this has all been so hard on her—more so than on anyone else. Naturally—her dearest brother killed, and her husband nearly killed, and I think she's…

Journal Entry (pp. 46-47)

…still not sure he'll pull through. I do think of her constantly. Woke up a couple times in the night, and then, about 5 am, I prayed especially for her and Arosa. (I'm sleeping better these nights since we got word that Tariri is still alive.)

Doris says Shimbotka ran away to Shutka's, though he was not with them at the killing. He left his wife and children, but Doris says they expect he'll come back to them and join the others. I suppose he's scared they'll retaliate against him, but Doris says there's no talk of killing him since he's related to them. There's no talk of retaliation at all in this group, she says, they just want to get away from it all. I'm surely glad to hear that. I hope it continues that way. I'm glad Shimbotka went up there. Now when he comes back, we can hear from him the reasons they gave for the killing and their reactions—if they were jubilant, or sad. Arosa's reactions. What Inchi had to say. I trust he will come back. If he can just trust this crowd…

Journal Entry (pp. 48-49)

…and believe they won't kill him; he can be an important link between the two groups. He can go back and forth, and we can keep some sort of contact.

Today I read Psalm 34, which again starts with praise. I do praise Him for all His goodness. Verses 4 and 5 are good.

Verse 7 surely applies to Tariri. *The angel of the Lord encamps around those who fear Him, and delivers them.* And verse 8 also. Verses 9 and 10 for the hungry, homeless Shapras: *O fear the Lord, you His saints, for those who fear him have no want! The young lions suffer want and hunger; but those who seek the Lord lack no good thing.* Verses 15 and 17. Verse 18 is for Irina and Arosa. Then verse 19: *Many are the afflictions of the righteous; but the Lord delivers him out of them all.*

Later today I was thinking, "If someone had to be killed, why Chiriapa? He's one I would have spared. Though our…

Journal Entry (pp. 49-50)

…newest believer, he was one of our most promising men believers to me—so sweet, and free from vice. I expected him to be a good testimony, and to be a real pal to the chief, and a help to him in standing by him.

I think Chiriapa got along better with the chief than anyone, and Arosa and Irina had become good friends—they, who once hated each other so much. But then the thought came to me. If someone had to be taken to accomplish the purpose of the Lord—perhaps Chiriapa was the readiest to enter His presence. Or if Satan had gained the victory in the lives of those people upriver (and our lives and prayers were not such to stem the tide) and it was inevitable that someone would be killed, perhaps the Lord said to Satan, "Let it be Chiriapa, he's ready to enter My presence." Though he was the newest believer, he was far ahead of some of the older ones. Perhaps he actually received the Lord in his heart before our last night there, when Doris dealt with him. She had been pointing out before he professed salvation, that he wanted a different kind of life—he'd stopped getting drunk, when they had *fiestas*, he didn't take part and he was just different. He didn't go around being rowdy or indulging in a lot of filthy talk. His attitude was different. His attitude toward the Word of God was always receptive. He was sweet and gentle.

Before, he was rough and rowdy and kind of like that wild crowd living with them for years up there after he married Arosa, but he had changed recently. He had more reason than some to talk of killing and hating, since his life was often sought, but he didn't talk like that. There seemed to be no bitterness or hatred in his heart. I would not have chosen him to be taken. I had great hopes for him. If it had been my choice, there would have been others I would have let go. But then, who am I to have a choice between life and death for someone else? Or even for myself? There are others less worthy to live. But who am I to say?

Perhaps that's not the way to look at it. Perhaps it was—who was worthy to die? But who am I to say? Only God can choose life and death. I hadn't thought of it at first, but I was thinking today that there has been no talk of killing, or persecution, because of the Gospel, perhaps that does enter in this situation. Perhaps it was not only an outburst of Satan against the work of the Gospel among the Shapras, but perhaps it was a deliberate attempt on the part of the upriver gang to stifle the voice of testimony—against their wicked lives and the Gospel.

Or if it was not consciously against it, perhaps it was unconsciously. What other reason could they have for killing Tariri? I've thought, "How could they kill him when he's so sweetly witnessed to them?" And his attitude seemed to be humble and loving. He gave them gifts in love, and shown such friendliness and tried to win them over. How could they turn on that and try to kill him? Perhaps that was their answer. They don't want it. Yet I'm not sure that they all don't want it. I'm not sure that Pinchu really wants to turn his back on the Lord. Shutka, Pirocha, and Chiriapa have at sometimes since Wau(tista's) death shown some interest in the Gospel, or conviction of sin. I believe it was genuine—because it was not natural.

It was against what they would ordinarily do, and in each circumstance, it was with others looking on jeering, or showing a definite disregard for the Word. Inchi hates the Word of God, I know, and anything to do with the Gospel. She has continually fought it all she could. And since Wautista's and Tayaanta's death, and Toripi's near escape, Toripi has had no interest, and has been antagonistic ever since.

Pirocha, though he has softened a few times toward the Gospel, has always sided with his mother in anything she wanted, it seems. Chiriapau (young Chiriapa), though interested, at times is kind of neutral, I think, and not strong either one way or the other. I don't think he especially wanted to kill, but he'd follow the crowd under pressure.

That leaves old Shutka and Pinchu. Pinchu, a young weak Christian who has been trying to buck the tribe—but is like a poor swimmer against a strong current—could easily give in. Perhaps he has tried to stand true, but what does he have to stand on? No written Word to feed on. Up there he has not even been hearing the Word, nor had fellowship with a group of believers. Just he and Yámpisa praying before meals with laughter ringing in their ears, and then prayer before bed and maybe in the morning. Singing together once in a while. He'd tried to refuse to take part in killings, but they shamed him into it. I think they've deliberately made him take a leading part to cure him.

Then there's old Shutka, who has shown a definite interest both when we talked to him, and when Pinchu did. When Pinchu did, Shutka, and Pirocha were sad, while Inchi laughed and raved about the lies. When we read and talked to Shutka, on…

Read Psalm 32 this morning. Verses 6 and…

PHOTOS

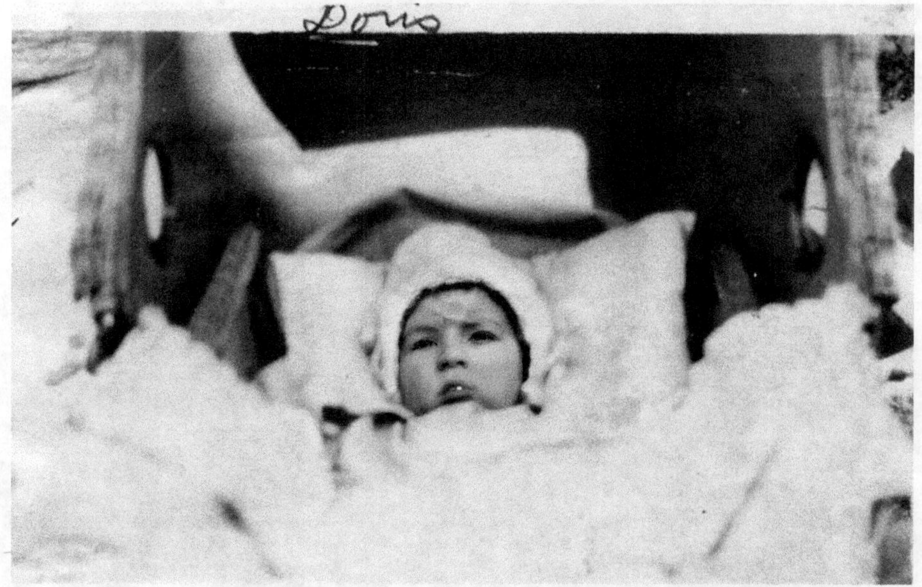

Lorrie Anderson as a baby. Winter of 1923

Young Lorrie Anderson

Lorrie and her pet dog

Lorrie Anderson at home at Christmas time

DORIS ANDERSON, by means of a 24 hour one-stop plane trip, on October 6 will land in Lima, Peru. She will be sent into the jungle to an aboriginal Indian tribe to learn the tribal dialect, reduce it to writing, and translate Scripture portions for the tribe.

Assisted by Mrs. Bessie Muller, she assembled and packed her equipment in the basement of our Missionary Home. Hundreds of items were given by friends in Hawthorne and elsewhere. We thought you would like to see her busy at the task. Here she is:

Lorrie Anderson and two Shapra women

Lorrie Anderson and a Shapra little girl

JAARS Jungle base at Yarinacocha, Peru – 1960s. Seven Helio Courier aircraft, three on pontoons (two on the river and one in front of the hangar); and two PBY Catalinas (the one on the right missing an engine) were stationed here.

One of the two PBY Catalinas being lowered to lake Yarinacocha before a flight to Purus.

Lorrie Anderson at the radio post in Pushaga

Lorrie and two Shapra children after a flight from Pushaga to Yarinacocha.

Antariya, Tariri's daughter, preparing *masato*.   Shutka with a little bird on his hand.

Thatched hut where Chief Tariri and Irina lived. On the right, the mosquito nets.

Chief Tariri and his family at Jungle Base Yarinacocha, about 1957. Back row: Mayanchi, Irina holding baby Arosa, Tariri, Tsirimpo. Front row: Antariya, Matarina, Totarika, Oroshpa.

Chief Tariri in his trip to Lima, Peru's capital, to visit Peruvian President General Manuel Odría. 1955

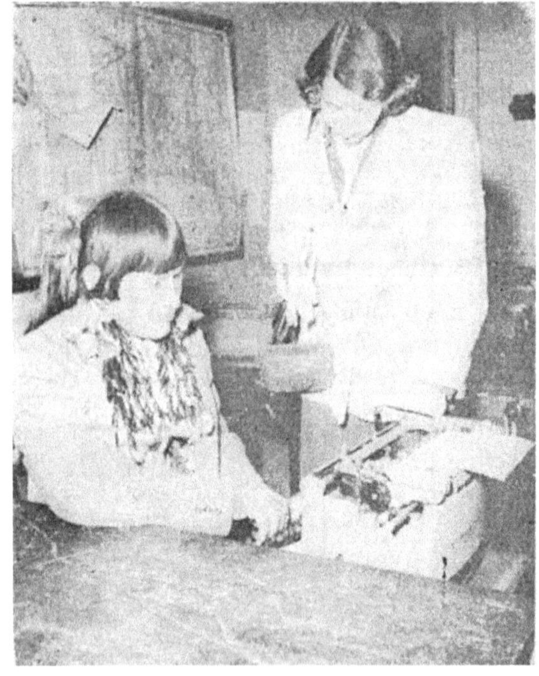

Lorrie shows Chief Tariri a typewriter, during their visit to the offices of the Peruvian newspaper *El Comercio,* Lima, 1955

Lorrie in home furloughs

www.ingramcontent.com/pod-product-compliance
Lightning Source LLC
Chambersburg PA
CBHW061529120726
48001CB00004B/1461